DAN SMITH

An Autobiography

ORIEL PRESS

© T. Dan Smith 1970
First Published 1970
ISBN O 85362 095 4
Library of Congress Catalogue Card Number 70 130030

Published by
ORIEL PRESS LTD.
32 Ridley Place
Newcastle-upon-Tyne NE1 8LH England

Text set in 11/13 point Baskerville
Printed in Great Britain by Bell & Bain Ltd. Glasgow C.1

Contents

I

CHILDHOOD

HOLLY AVENUE runs like a gash across the centre of Wallsend. Dead straight and south facing, it cuts an east-west trough across terraces of similar industrial boxes. On one side of Holly Avenue is a row of low-slung two-storey red brick houses which crouch defensively over serried ranks of doors. Endless doors it seems, for these are up-and-down flats. Under the grey slate roofs Holly Avenue must have always packed in more than its fair share of humanity. A good combination, I always thought, of pretending that every man's home was his castle and playing a real life game of sardines.

I lived at number 62, in a ground floor flat. One of my earliest memories is of looking out through the front room window across the narrow cobbled expanse of Holly Avenue and being somehow surprised to find on the opposite side of the street not a duplicate of my house, as one was accustomed to seeing in Wallsend, but a railway embankment. For on the opposite side of Holly Avenue there was the electric railway, striding superb and shining from Newcastle to the coast. Both of these places seemed very distant to me in my young days because I did not come from a much-travelled family. A hundred yards for shopping, a couple of hundred yards to the church, made up much of my world. It was a place where the majority of the families who survived the 1914–1918 war were born, reared, worked, married, grew old and died.

In a sense, although quite a large town, it retained its village atmosphere. And of course from my earliest days I was made to feel proud of Wallsend. After all, this was where the Romans decided that they would end their wall—Segedunum they called it. In the Richardson Dees Park at Wallsend, a haven of greenness and peace in that industrial town, the end of that wall had been reconstructed. I used to make pilgrimages there with my mother to read the inscription and to feed the swans on the lake. Then again, just over the railway embankment, and I could just glimpse this by craning my neck upwards from our front room window, were the tall cranes and the ceaseless noise of hammers which were familiar to all of us in our riverside residences. Swan Hunters and the other large shipyards, those proud spawners of giants such as the Mauretania and, more recently, the Esso Northumbria, were sources of pride to us. We knew somehow, even in our young ingenuousness, that we were part of a rather magnificent tradition of workmanship.

My own father was not connected with the shipyards, but rather with the other staple industry of Wallsend, which was coal mining. He had originally been a Durham miner. He came from Durham stock and among the odd things that he left behind when he died and which I still have, there is a book written by his father; not significantly written, but nevertheless indicating that my grandfather was a reasonably intelligent man. He had been born in 1848, and that he could write indicated a certain amount of intelligence. His wife, that is my grandmother, is equally discernible in the same book as being a woman who could hardly write her name. I am turning over the pages now, and there I can see line after line of 'Mary Ann Smith' laboriously scrawled by her. At the same time, her wedding certificate was signed with a cross. There was, then, in this alliance of my grandparents, a certain amount of learning and a fair amount of ignorance, and this combination came through in my father as I knew him. He was, on the whole, very well read. He was always reading. In the main he favoured books of some importance. He never read a novel unless he wanted to laugh ; then he would turn to 'Three Men in a Boat' or Mark Twain's 'Innocents Abroad'. Very often he would turn to light travel books. I remember that H. V. Morton was one of the authors with whom I was brought up. When my father lived in Durham, working in the mining industry, he was intensely political and was always a rebel. At all times he was on the side of the rebels. He looked with great admiration on the early Clydeside workers who fought for their rights. Those who were his friends were people whom I came to know as shadowy figures in my early days. He always held them in high esteem and he considered that anyone who did not stick up for socialist beliefs was a traitor. His political thoughts were ahead of their time. He was a European. He thought and talked a lot about the united socialist states of Europe and was tremendously impressed by the achievements of Russia. Even from my earliest days it seemed to me in fact that these were the achievements of a dictatorship, but my father had the blind spot of many men of his time, who saw in the Russian Revolution the dawn of a new democratic era, and tended to gloss over what I considered to be the shortcomings of the regime. For all that he was a sensitive man, he did not ever see those things which happened in Russia as being other than explicable and excusable in terms of the deplorable economic conditions of its people. Therefore he could justify almost anything, believing that in the long run liberty would come ; liberty was just around the corner. My father was also interested in music. Even though he did not come from a musical family he would spend hours and hours by the piano fingering the keys, and another of my boyhood recollections is of the tall-back, old-fashioned piano occupying a quite un-justifiably large area of our small living room. He was also enthusiastic about playing gramophone records, bought second-hand or given to him by one of the lodgers my mother took in. I remember a record of Caruso and another one of Clara Butt, scratching along. As the gaslighter passed outside the window on dim frosty winter evenings I would sprawl in an armchair listening to the needle scratching its way amongst the grooves, interrupted from time to time by the screech and hiss of an electric train as it made its way from one end of the earth—or so it seemed to me—to the other.

My mother encouraged me in my early acquaintance with music. She was very different from my father, coming from Cumbrian farming stock. She always boasted that she was a Clifford. My sister in particular would recall that our family went back to Lady Anne Clifford, Countess of Dorset. Little good it did us in our humble terrace house stuck there in the middle of Holly Avenue with never a holly bush, or anything at all redolent of the countryside to remind us of our ancestor, Lady Anne. My mother seemed to have those qualities of hard work which are typical of the Cumbrian fell farmer. She was a cultured woman, and this culture expressed itself in good manners and an appreciation of what one used to call in those days courtesy. She was interested in the way that my sister and I ate our food, the way in which we put down our knives and forks and the way in which we folded our table napkins. She was interested in cleanliness and the preparation of meals. To her these things were very important. In addition to that, she was religious and this was the background to her socialist convictions. She was a Christian Socialist and she had infinite courage. It was difficult in those days to make ends meet. I remember her excitement when Sir Patrick Hastings won Wallsend constituency for the first time as a Labour Member of Parliament. It seemed that good times were just over the horizon. My mother was a keen supporter of Sir Patrick, and I can recall a certain tension in the house at that time because my mother had tremendous strength of character verging on obstinacy and my father, while dedicated to the communist cause, was in many ways a weak man. One might have described him as a waverer. Many times I have wondered what bond there was that kept my father and mother so close together. My father had in many ways the worst features of a Durham miner. He was a gambler ; he liked to drink. My mother hated both intensely, so that there was, as a tapestry, lying round the walls of my small but snug house, this conflict which worried me a little. Yet there was also the political cement that bound them together in something that was, I think, bigger than both of them.

I was born in 1915. At an early age I became interested in religion, largely because my mother insisted I went to church. I remember the walk in my Sunday best along with my sister, up on to the High Street at Wallsend, along by the tall gaunt Richardson Dees school, with the smoking chimneys and the skyscraper cranes looming at us from the river. Part of our regular footslogging journey took us through areas of Wallsend which were quite rustic, and our destination was St Peter's Church at the east end of the town. It was a pleasant, grimy building surrounded by a churchyard. I was interested in reading the names on the tombstones as I trailed my way regularly across to the church. Canon Osborne was the vicar, and he was a socialist. He was not terribly popular, but he was a well-known figure and impressed me tremendously with what I was pleased to call his speeches. My father went to church, not to listen to the sermon, but because he liked singing. He had a good singing voice with a remarkable range, and was a member of the choir. In my early boyhood days I also got pleasure from singing. I never felt that I wanted to be one of the chorus though. If I was going to sing, then I had to be a very good singer, so while I still had my boy's voice both at school and church, I used to work at my singing. My sister played the piano and understood music and I could read music to a certain extent. I lay no claim to be a musician, but I can now, and I could then, sing from music. My boyhood vocal hero was Ernest Lough who used to sing 'Oh for the Wings of a Dove' and 'I Know that My Redeemer Liveth', and I used to listen to these on my scratchy gramophone, practise them sometimes in front of a mirror, and promise myself that some day St Peter's church would echo to my own soprano voice emulating Master Lough. It never quite happened.

I went to school in 1920. I can still recall the first day. My mother took me by the hand and, all smartened and scrubbed, I was led somewhat reluctantly past the Wallsend Baths, up on to the High Street by the clanking tramcars, into the Richardson Dees Infants' School. It reminded me, on that rather terrifying day, of a penitentiary. There it stood, red brick and surrounded by iron railings, with a vast expanse of concrete separating the familiar road from the unfamiliar new world. The smell of chalk and dust and sweat remain in my nostrils now, and the tension of that day is still with me. But somehow four o'clock came and for the rest of my time in the Richardson Dees I was pleasantly, if not brilliantly, stimulated. There is only one teacher whom I can recall. She was the person who first opened my eyes to drawing and painting. After a year or two I moved to the Central School. I learned to read and write and do sums, but school was not really a dominant influence in my young life. Rather it was the sight of unemployed men playing quoits on the expanse of waste land opposite the Town Hall, or the queues outside the Labour Exchange, or the ignominy of having to join the boot queue on the occasion when I just had no shoes suitable for wearing. Because in the early 1920's my father found himself several times on the dole. A miner's life was in those days unpredictable. He had started work in Wallsend at the G Pit, and when it finished, he finished. So there were many periods when things got slack and when he found himself with the other men standing at the street corners.

In 1926 he was offered a pit house at the west end of the town in Portugal Place. This had the advantage of being rent free and included the perk of free coal; that was, when he was working. I do not know how Portugal Place got its name but it was certainly an interesting place. Opposite my house was a mortuary and a gentlemen's toilet and the corporation refuse yard. In those days the toilets were non-flush. My mother's hygenic susceptibilities were offended and she indulged in several crusades directed towards cleaning up the area. The stream of lorries which used to come from time to time to 'do out' the old middens was certainly no great attraction, but I must admit that the mortuary remained for me a source of fascination.

I was now in my teens and attended the Western Boys' School. This was on the outskirts of the town. I remember that one could climb to the top of the high playground wall and look out on to fields and allotments. The children who attended this school were a fair cross section of the limited social stratum of the town, and with heightening awareness I was able to perceive that the tradesmen's sons coming from homes where there were books, and where there were parents at least marginally interested in education, were able to perform more competently in the classroom. Not that the demands made upon any of us were very great. The three 'Rs' were still predominant, discipline was quite rigid, and personal development was not encouraged. Those of us who, like myself, had mastered the basic techniques, were elevated to the status of monitor. In effect this meant that we spent most of our time giving out the milk, running messages, collecting money for saving stamps and mixing the ink. After the age of eleven, when I had failed the 'scholarship,' I was never really stretched. I am not quite sure why I did not pass the exam for the secondary school at Wallsend. I suspect it was both because I was nervous and also because I was not motivated to do so. I remember thinking, whilst at the Western School, that it seemed very strange that one spent one's days within a place nominally dedicated to study and yet found so little of interest to engage one. It was still my books at home and my gramophone records, and now more and more my interest in what was going on socially around me, which engaged my attention. Art at school, which in the 1920's was still a very formal discipline, was killed for me by teachers who expressed the opinion that I possessed no talent. How very different it must be nowadays when one can see with what joy most children express themselves in varying forms on paper. The rising generation may have much to protest about, but at the same time it also has a great deal to be thankful for in its education system. Looking back, I do not think that I showed much power of leadership in my school days. Only in music did I want to forge ahead, and even here if one was

engaged in 'We Three Kings of Orient', then while I would be
keen to be one of the kings, it was unlikely that I would ever
have aspired to be the sole king. One of my teachers, called
Smith, did try to encourage my interest in music, and went
beyond what would be considered to be a teacher's duty in
those days. He used to play Beethoven and Mozart and talk to
me about those composers and about the pleasures of listening
to classical music.

But those were hard days. School, even though a sterile place
as compared with today, was still an oasis in a grim social
situation. My father was out of work a lot. My mother had two
jobs. She helped to clean the telephone exchange at Wallsend
and also the Shell Oil Company offices in Newcastle. Leaving
home at six in the morning, and walking several hundred yards
in order to save a ha'penny tram car fare, she would do her
first job, and in the evening there would be the second round of
cleaning to undertake. With the wages which she earned, she
not only fed us and clothed us reasonably well, but also bought
a new piano and encouraged both my sister and me to work
hard at our music. All this, of course, wore her out. She
burned herself out. She did not live long after the end of the
second world war. Just long enough to have one run in the first
car that I ever bought. She was ambitious for me in the way
that mothers in humble families often are. I still remember her
pride when Thomas Daniel Smith was chosen to give the fare-
well speech on behalf of the pupils at the Western School, when
Mr Tocker, the headmaster, retired. What a lot of practising
I had to do, under the supervision of both my mother and my
sister. I had to learn to pronounce the words of my oration
clearly. I had to practise forming sounds in my throat and I can
still remember the opening words, 'Mr. Tocker, teachers and
boys. It is an honour . . .' I could imagine the lads at the back
of the hall whispering to each other, 'Listen to wor Dan, putting
his posh voice on.'

My spare time pursuits, whilst I lived at Portugal Place, were
not entirely cultural. They were largely determined by the

environment. Very often, I used to go to Hedley's Corner which was the Speaker's Corner of Wallsend, and listen to Jimmy Stewart. He was the sort of character in the Labour movement in Wallsend then, who could draw a crowd. He used to be up on his soapbox and holding us all spellbound. I have subsequently spoken at Hedley's Corner many times myself. Then there was the Borough Field at Wallsend too. This was a large expanse of land on which stalls used to be set up to offer cheapjack goods on weekdays whilst on Sunday evenings the politicians and the evangelists used to enthrall me. Another of my leisure-time pursuits was centred on two nearby slaughter houses, one owned by Thornton the butcher on the High Street, and another by Smith, who had a shop near to the Presbyterian Church. Wallsend butchers used to slaughter their own beasts in those days, and I remember a regular Monday date for me was to watch the cattle being driven into Wallsend, starting off at the top of the long straight High Street. There they would be, some dozen of them, panic-stricken and trembling, a sad sight in fact, but to me, in my teens, in days when adventure was at a premium, it was like a wild west rodeo. They would be led, two by two, into the slaughter house, and I could see the fear in their faces. I would watch them being killed. Eventually I came to quite enjoy it, and this, as I see it, is one of the dangers of living in a deprived environment. One becomes accustomed to the sordidness and the depravity of it all. After the beasts were killed, we used to go and beg for cows' bladders, blow them up, and play 'heids on' with them. My mother used to be disgusted with all this, but I suspect that my father was not entirely disapproving.

As a rebel, he left his own imprint on my boyhood days. For instance, he adjured me sternly never to stand for the National Anthem, and when we had our Empire Day parades, when the whole school mustered in the playground and all boys proudly wore their fathers' medals and saluted the flag, I used to go bereft of medals and with the guilty feeling that I really shouldn't enjoy singing the patriotic songs. Secretly I was a little envious of my colleagues. One day I discovered a medallion in the chest of drawers. I do not know what it was for. For all I know it may have been for loyal service to socialist causes. Anyhow, I went to school wearing it and feeling inordinately proud. I remember one of the teachers stopping me, looking at it carefully, and then regarding me quizzically. Rather decently, he passed no comment.

But how can I be other than grateful to my father? It was he who introduced me to Caruso and Clara Butt. It was he who opened my eyes to Plato's Republic, and would discuss with me as a young, ill-informed boy, the philosophies of Marx and Plato, and the writings of H. G. Wells and Bernard Shaw. When there was a little money in the house, he would be the one who would take me to the People's Theatre, or to see Chaliapin perform at the City Hall. I remember one concert which we attended there, when the hall was almost empty, and the great musician came to the front of the stage and invited us all to come up into the front seats. And I recall that my father, with his catholic taste in music, would also take me along to the Empire Theatre in Newcastle where the more popular entertainers of the twenties and early thirties were to be seen. I later recall seeing Louis Armstrong give one of his earliest performances in Newcastle. He was booed off the stage. I really do not think that Newcastle was quite ready for Louis' expertise. The audiences at the Empire went to see variety concerts, and the local press was hostile to this 'pouty-lipped man, slavering into his trumpet'.

Most people can look back to a confusion in their formative years. Certainly I can. The roughness and earthiness of the provincial industrial town, the Geordie clarion cry of 'Howway the lads', at every street-corner football game, the strident good humour of a generation of men thrown on the scrapheap. All this is inextricably mixed in my mind with the graciousness of gaslit afternoons, with Schubert being played on the piano, delicately-sliced bread, and George Bernard Shaw on the sideboard. It was a good beginning.

2

DOLE DAYS

IT WAS a dark November morning, seven o'clock, with a cold
wind biting its way along the Tyne. A thin drizzle was falling.
The droplets of rain gathered on my hair, rolled over my fore-
head and down across my nose. My fingers were numb and I
kept moving from one foot to the other to induce a little cir-
culation. My eyes were half-full of sleep and my blood ran thin.
It was like keeping company with an iceberg. I was thirteen
years old and I was standing outside Swan's Shipyard at
Wallsend. In a couple of months time I was due to leave school
and I had come specially this morning to see what the staple
industry of my home town was likely to be able to offer me.
The omens were not good. A knot of shadowy figures was
gathering around me. This was the custom in 1928. Those who
were looking for work came, rather like slaves to the market, to
foregather in the early morning and wait for the imperious
command either to come in or to 'Gan off te the Labour'. The
minutes passed, the wind continued to blow, and the luckier
people who were actually working in the yard began to clatter
their way down the steep cobbled streets towards the yard.
Through the gates they went, punching-in and becoming lost
in the murk. 7.30 arrived and now there was a crowd of about
a hundred of us gathered outside the gates. Suddenly the blast
of a work's buzzer shattered the stillness. Then another, and still
another, until for the space of about ten seconds there was a
virtual chorus, ear-splitting itself along the river. In one sense
it was a symphony, overpowering and majestic, and repeated
at this time every day. But to me on that morning it was frighten-

ing. For the first time I think I realised that big lad though I was (I'm over six feet now), I was, as an individual, only a terribly small and insignificant cog in a huge, demanding, remorseless machine. It was perhaps my first-ever confrontation as an individual with 'the system'.

I did not get a job at Swan's but, when I left school, I signed on at the 'Labour' and started looking around myself. There were no organisations like career guidance in those days, and my parents were not really qualified to guide me greatly. I had to go looking for myself. Eventually I decided to take the first job that came along, as a painter's apprentice in Wallsend. I suppose I must have been a reasonably keen, bright-looking lad, or at least I must have appeared so against the background of the average run of boys in Wallsend. They cannot have been other than rather down-at-heel, whereas those of us who had parents who cared, at least had clothes that were darned and patched, and shoes which had a fair lick of polish on them. The name of my employer was Ralph Moore. Stan Moore, his son, was very good to me. When one considers that I had been told at school that I was no good with a brush in my hand, it was really a bit of cheek for me to expect to earn my livelihood by painting. Stan was a skilled worker and he was keen for me to get on. I was paid 4/10d a week, which contributed to the housekeeping budget and helped me to eat and buy overalls. Stan thought that it would be a good idea for me to attend evening classes, and therefore I went to Rutherford College which helped me to bridge the adolescent gap between the harsh reality of working at a rather humdrum job, and the necessity to come to grips with myself as a person. I may have lived in Portugal Place, but at least on Monday nights I could spend some time dreaming my way through Rome and Athens. I may have spent eight hours a day slapping paint on to buildings, but for a few precious hours each week I could wander the maze of Corinthian, Doric and Ionic pillars. Then I had to make the first important, solitary decision of my life. I decided that although Stan Moore had been extremely good to me, my prospects in Wallsend as a painter and decorator were limited. So I went to my boss and told him I had decided to leave and go to work for a firm in Newcastle. He was annoyed. It was a hard decision to make. It was perhaps the first time that I have ever felt lonely, but then, you see, I just did not have anyone to guide me. I could see no career ladder stretching before me. It was me against the world.

The new firm of painters that employed me was based in Orchard Street in Newcastle, and the year was 1930. At that time, there was a lot of painting to be done for our Tyneside newspaper, the *Evening Chronicle*, and shortly afterwards there burst on the North a rival paper called the *Evening World*. My boss changed allegiance, and I spent a hectic time going round the paper's branches and newsagents' shops throughout the north painting 'Evening World' in gold and black letters on bright red shops. The other apprentices I worked with were good lads but, again, I could sense that because I was the sort of person I was, I tended to be a little apart from them. For instance, I have never all my life enjoyed dirty jokes. I am not interested in hearing these from anyone. My pals used to bring pornographic picture cards along to the jobs they were doing, but I could show no enthusiasm for these. I do not think that I am a puritan; I do not think that I am a spoilsport; I am certainly not a religious man. I am liberal in my attitude towards the freeing of literature and the theatre from censorship, but to go a party in London as I did some years ago, and find the first item on the agenda to be the showing of a blue film, affronted me. I said to my host 'I'm sorry, I don't know what kind of a person you think I am, but as far as I'm concerned I'm leaving now,' and I put on my coat and went out of the door. I was the same at the age of fifteen. It would have been much easier to conform and give a belly-laugh, but I like to think that this is when a certain amount of character began to show in myself, and it might even have been the first time that I began to sense that I might have certain powers of leadership.

Be that as it may, powers of leadership were not much help

to me when the 'Evening World' went out of business and my painting firm found itself without a contract and with gallons of red and black paint. I remember that I was working on a branch at Bishop Auckland at the time. I was sixteen years of age and I was out of work. 'Oh dear,' I thought, 'This isn't very good.' At that time the authorities had introduced a system of dole schools. The philosophy behind these institutions was at that time difficult for me to understand. It seemed, in general, to result in painters' apprentices like myself having to learn how to cut somebody's hair or how to become a joiner. I could see neither sense nor reason in it at all. However, I had no money so I fell in with the system. I joined a woodwork class and produced a large number of extremely ugly and functionless articles. My dole school was at Jarrow, and I had to walk from my home in Portugal Place to the ferry, cross the river, and wander into what was to me a place of unmitigated misery. I hated every minute of it as a futile waste of time. I was not allowed to do anything, or to read anything, which was of any interest to me. However, the lads and I used to have our jokes. We used to say that rather than being educated at Eton and Harrow, we were receiving our upbringing at Heaton and Jarrow.

For three years I was in and out of work. In fact, even when I was working I really could not see the point of it, because all my earnings were taken away from me. Those were the days of the means test, and what I contributed to the family income was deducted from my father's public assistance money. I felt humiliated. I remember thinking, 'Isn't it strange how these folks who believe in enterprise, and in individuals getting on, could create this kind of situation?' At the same time, while I had continued attending church in Wallsend, first of all at Bigges' Main which was near to my home at Portugal Place, and later at St. John's, I began to be disillusioned. There were still one or two clergymen, like a Donald Cooper whom I recall, who was a tremendously passionate campaigner against injustice; there were still one or two of his ilk who could inspire me, but I could not help feeling that here I was in a society which was economically undermining the human spirit, and this brought no protest from the church. Singing hymns I enjoyed. Christian Socialism meant less and less to me.

Although life was grey and restricted in the early thirties, it was not uniformly so. Geordie is a remarkable character. He is possessed of a resilience and an optimism which rubs off on his environment. So the Richardson Dees park at Wallsend glowed warm on summer evenings when the pit bands delighted us. Jakey the swan, tiring of his quagmire of a lake, would stroll down Park Road, stop the traffic in the High Street, and give us a talking point for days on end. On winter nights there was 'A fish and a pennorth with a lot of batter, missis' and a three-penny wooden tip-up seat in the fleapit Borough Cinema, where Charlie Chaplin once played—live! Although a grimy, close-packed town of over 30,000 people, Wallsend kept its village atmosphere. Mr Brewis, grizzly-bearded and bowler-hatted, drove his horse and trap from his urban farm to deliver milk, warm and sweet from the churn, to our doors. The lime trees drooped heavy in Ferndale Avenue on July days that went on for ever. And if I spent some of those days squatting on my hunkers near the 'Labour', they were none-the-less serene and, in a sense, stimulating days. There was time to think and to dream.

It was in 1935 that I met my wife-to-be. Her formal schooling had been similar to mine, but she was exceptionally well read. To this day her wide range of knowledge astonishes me. While I fumble my way through Bamber Gascoigne's T.V. teasers, she seems to rattle off the answers without effort. And there we were in love, with a few bob in the Penny Bank. My socialism was bubbling over—Marx, Engels and Kant rubbed shoulders with me from breakfast time through to signing-off time on 2LO, whereas for Ada it was literature, the theatre and ballet—all unexplored territory to me. And so the cranes and the chimneys, the pit heaps and the dry middens, the dole and the degradation, all became bearable and fell into perspective. It was like turning the page of a book.

3

A PLAGUE ON THEM

MY HOME now is a terrace house in Newcastle. Looking out over the Leazes Moor, towards the city skyline, it is, I suppose, what estate agents would call 'conveniently situated'. From my sitting-room window I can see St. James' Park, where Newcastle United pursue a love-hate relationship with their many fans. I am one of them. A season ticket to every home game is a must for me. The black and white of the Magpies, so satisfying in its consummation of opposites, is for me a symbol of the successes and failures of the 'canny toon'.

In retrospect I see the 1930's in political terms as a black and white period in my life. There was no argument about the inequalities, the poverty and the effects of poverty, because one lived through these and was affected by them. But on the wider issues of fascism, nazi-ism and politics in general, and on the different policies of Russia, or Germany, or Spain, or Italy, one was brought face to face with attitudes to war and I felt that I had to get my thinking clear on this issue. For the whole of the 30's, literally from being fourteen years of age until the 1939 war came, I was involved in an on-going argument within my own mind as to what were the rights and wrongs of the international situation. I weighed courses of action and argued wherever I went and with whomever I talked. I was never in company without getting quickly on to a discussion of political issues.

My wife, basically, was non-political. Her family was split. She had an uncle who was a Labour Party supporter, but she was an east end of Newcastle girl and those were the days of Robert Aske, 'Tea-party Bob' the Liberal M.P. Her folk were mainly Robert Aske Liberals.

I went through the stage of attending W.E.A. classes on international affairs. One teacher who particularly impressed me was a fellow called Nightingale. We had tremendous discussions, debates and arguments. These were under the auspices of the International Friendship League, an organisation which at that time had been set up, theoretically at least, to foster international friendship. I remember when war broke out, the international friendship went out quicker than the war came in. People who had felt a great deal about each other suddenly decided that they had nothing in common. Ted Short was a leading member of the International Friendship League and was even then a very skilled debater. More often than not, he and I would disagree, but I had a tremendously high regard for him, for his ability and energy, and it did not surprise me when he eventually blossomed forth in politics.

Then I resolved my own thinking on war, and became one of the founder members of the Peace Pledge Union. Dick Shepherd was the man who founded the movement and brought out the pledge, 'We renounce war and pledge ourselves never to take part in it.' He came north to meet a few of us. I remember there was Large the printer, Sadler of Byker and, I think, Richardson of a leather firm. There were half a dozen of us who met in Mundella Terrace at Heaton. Old Jack Sadler had been a conscientious objector in the first world war and we took it upon ourselves to organise, as best we could the Peace Pledge Union in the North. We were excited by the current Oxford Students' Union debate in which a resolution renouncing war had been passed. I felt that this was a critical point of time because although I was becoming disillusioned about the church, I believed fervently that Christ would not have gone to war; Christ would not have tolerated bloodshed. It was very much that kind of fervour which directed me to the Peace Pledge Union. I felt that I would be strong enough, if it came to the crunch, to reject a military solution to any problem. So the black and white of things fell into place for me.

I suppose the issue was a communist versus fascist one, and in North-East England there developed a centre of practical activity. I found myself in touch with a lot of Czech refugees and Basque children who had been left without parents during the Spanish War. It was a period of international politics, with the threat of major war for the first time being felt closely by the people of Britain. In the mid-thirties there was the word 'Guernica' which entered everyone's vocabulary and remained an evocative word until 'Hiroshima' replaced it, and from my early days my political leanings were not only left-wing and anti-fascist, but hostile to people who were in any way sympathetic to fascism. I remember regularly quoting at that time what I considered to be one of Churchill's major speeches in support of fasicm. He had made it at a meeting on behalf of the Italian fascists in 1923. It went something like this : 'If I had been an Italian, I would have been whole-heartedly with you in this struggle against the bestial appetites and passions of Leninism.' This set me back on my heels. But likewise, from my place in the dole queue, I could see no great merit in communism either. As far as I was concerned, politics boiled down to a struggle for the liberty of the individual, and my own inclination politically was to say, 'A plague on both your houses.' This was why I became a pacifist and socialist.

It was clear to me, when I joined Dick Shepherd's protest movement of the thirties, that war was inevitable. Most of my energies were taken up with anti-war campaigning, but I had the confusion of the time in my mind, namely : could there be good wars ? The anti-fascist Spaniards, were I felt, involved in a good kind of war. It was an anti-fascist war and I tended to support the Spanish people, although in political terms I was a supporter of what was called the POUM. This was a democratic socialist organisation. I had never been attracted to the communist party because I did not like the organisation or form that communism took. Whatever support in the way of political ideas I might have had for it were destroyed as a result of what happened to people whom I knew who were killed when they went to Spain to fight fascism. They were, in fact, killed by the Spanish communists because they were fighting for liberty rather than fighting for the triumph of Russian policy in Spain.

One of the things that I have thought a great deal about in the last decade is the proposition that assuming that the communist front had been successful in Spain and the Fascists had been defeated, and bearing in mind that in Italy and in France, the popular front, communist-dominated working class movement might also have taken power, would this in fact have been a march forward for freedom and the individual—or not? I believed then that it would. I do not now believe that. And so I look back at the political situation in the thirties as being only anti-comintern. There was no clear Socialist alternative on offer. Now this meant that when the war broke out in 1939, I had made up my mind that I really did not trust the politicians, who had been largely instrumental in helping the rise of fascism. These included Churchill, who in his early days saw this as an instrument in the battle against communism. Also Neville Chamberlain, and for that matter Ernie Bevin and some of his colleagues. These were not the men who would produce out of war the kind of society that I myself believed was the right one.

In this belief I was in good company. The democratic socialists, the libertarians, the Fenner Brockways, and the Maxtons, the dreamers, the Lansburies, Campbell Steven, Jimmy Carmichael, Buchanan, Jennie Lee, and others could not see the kind of society which we believed in, being at all realisable under the aegis of the people who were leading us in the war. It was a real dilemma, because one has got to remember that in the heat of the time, to be anti-war was not a popular line, and I was an outspoken anti-war person. We built up a unique war resistance movement in Newcastle. I carried on meetings in the open air and indoors and argued that ultimately the defeat of fascism and the kind of society that one sought to establish came back to the ability of political leaders to enthuse the people about causes for which people would be prepared to die. Good, positive causes, rather than to strike a pose like being anti-German. The politicians answered that line saying, 'Right, let's finish the Germans and we'll all be free.' My own view was, throughout the war, that while I could see that there was an undeniable argument, that if the Germans got here there would be concentration camps, and they would carry out repugnant policies, I felt that in the long term the real political victories could only be won if people were prepared to die for causes that were not necessarily military causes. I believe that still today.

So by the time the war had come to an end I felt that large areas of Europe had lost what freedom had survived until 1939, because as a 30-year-old in 1945, the only freedom that I felt I had enjoyed was the freedom to speak and to agitate, the freedom to read and to learn. And again, as far as I could see, any progress that had been made in Britain was as a result of ordinary people increasingly being aware of their own need to organise themselves into trade unions in order to fight against what were quite primitive working conditions. Looking at the trade union structure today, it is possible now, as then, to return to the root of the problem and say, 'How are we going to deal with the trade unions and get them to play a positive part in creating a new society?' And answer now, as then, 'Only by giving them the vision of a fine society which will get them away from the feeling that they are there to protest and the belief that they are in competition with the boss, be he private or state employer.' And I did not see that proposition being any more realisable than the equally improbable creation of a free society by the instruments of war. What happened at Hiroshima was a sort of warning to the Russians that the West had atomic weapons and therefore they had better settle up in the Far East.

Equally, in the trade union world, the threat of legislation and penal clauses now represent the Hiroshima of British capitalism. Trying to pretend that by dropping an atomic bomb you solve something is as make-believe as playing the game of solving industrial disputes by legislation. In fact one aggravates the problem. One creates a bigger monster than that which one is seeking to destroy. In a personal sense, of course, being anti-war brought one all the usual questions. 'What would happen if the Germans came and bayonetted your mother?' I remember having a discussion at the time with one or two pro-war people and I used to say, 'Well, look, if anyone came and bayonetted my mother I would possibly kill him. But the one thing you can depend on is that I won't bayonet your mother. Certainly if the Germans are worried about me coming to bayonet their mothers, they can count me out. You might go and do it.' I was prepared to die but not to kill. I feel that this point would sum up what I believe to be the responsibility of the individual.

You can only plan a society on what you yourself can do. You cannot plan a society on the basis that somebody is always going to do evil and that therefore it is necessary to be anti-evil rather than pro-good.

When the war ended then, I was disillusioned to put it mildly. I had taken an active part in politics and taken a minor part in the elections that were fought towards the end of the war. There was a coalition during the war and people had been denied the right to vote. All the political parties had vied with each other in sloganising. 'Open a second front'. 'Let's get on with the war more quickly'. 'Let's wipe the Germans off the face of the earth'. 'The only good German's a dead one'. All of this seemed to me then to be most irrelevant to the real problems that caused the war. My colleagues and I had been, wherever we could, trying in the Independent Labour Party to fight by-elections in order to give people an opportunity to express themselves on matters of public importance. In other words, what we were saying was, 'Are you going back to 1939? We may be wrong in saying you should be anti-war, but what we are concerned about is the kind of society which is going to stem from the victory that you

think you're going to win.' In the early days of the war we got
dusty answers.

I was helping in an election campaign in Edinburgh East
at the time when two British battleships were sunk by air attack
off Malaya. People were understandably more interested in the
sinking than they were in our political philosophy. One would
almost have thought on that cold day outside a factory that
we had sunk the battleships, instead of the Japanese. But later
in the war it became obvious that people were really concerned
about the kind of war they were fighting and were determined
that they were not going to return to the old days.

At the same time it was equally clear to me and my own
political colleagues that the major powers were beginning to
feel that the people they were fighting against were going to be
important allies in the next stage of what they called the anti-
comintern struggle. And so we talked, lightly I think, about
internationalism and the nonsense of calling all Japanese bad
and all Chinese good, and what were good things and what bad
things. When people were on our side it seemed they were good
and when on the other side they were bad. Out of this we were
trying, as we had been through the thirties and earlier than
that, to put forward the idea of a united Europe because this
had been the message from the early part of the century, that
the traditions and the culture of Europe were of supreme importance, that the two major powers, the Americans and the
Russians, really did not have the kind of political systems, or
the depths of tradition out of which could emerge what we were
calling a libertarian society. This concept was to us, the united
socialist states of Europe. This was the message we were trying
to get across at election time.

At the same time, there was a small contributory cloud which
remained small, and then eventually blew away. This was the
Commonwealth Movement under Sir Richard Acland, which
was also fighting to end the coalition and to give people an
opportunity to vote. The argument that was going on then in
political circles between the Tories and the Labour Party, and

what was at that stage left of the Liberal Party, did not include an awareness of the tremendous pressure for a general election. I know that at that time the Labour movement, and most of its leadership in particular, were far removed from the true feelings of the people. Like the Tory party, Parliamentary socialists believed that the wartime coalition could carry on for ever and that if it did, nobody would really protest. If by chance it was broken, people said, Winston Churchill would sweep back into power. Whereas I had become aware, because of my experience, of the deep-felt needs of ordinary people who were sick to death of living in the slums, whether they were in East Edinburgh, or in Bilston where Bob Edwards almost won a seat in a by-election for the I.L.P., or anywhere else. Wherever these by-elections were fought, there was this clear evidence that people did not want to go back to the kind of society that they had left behind in 1939, and that if the war was to yield anything at all, then it had to be the beginnings of a new society.

So I went through my period of disillusionment because so few politicians, until the results of the election were announced, could see the tremendous opportunities that presented themselves to leaders of courage. Here we had a Europe, razed in many places to the ground, presenting new opportunities, and if ever there was a time for Britain to go into Europe and give a lead, it was in those radical days in 1945. And yet it was only a matter of a couple of years after the election of Labour that the arguments were about petty things, like how much red meat do you get for your lunch, or what are you getting out of the system. So although gigantic strides were made in the health service and other fields, we began to fritter away the tremendous spiritual energy of the British people. The 'never-had-it-so-good' era had set in.

On the other hand of course many of the international ideals that we had been supporting in Newcastle and in the north generally were coming to fruition, because we had a strong movement in support of Indian independence. In the thirties, many of the people who were involved in the Indian and

African struggles had come to Britain and I used to meet
them at summer schools. Sometimes they would come to Newcastle. At that time the representative of the Indian League
in Newcastle, was Krishna Menon. Later he became War
Minister in the Indian government. There was also Jomo
Kenyatta who was in London for some years and who had a real
understanding of the people who were advocating the liberation
of Kenya. In Newcastle my colleagues and I took part in
building up the League against Imperialism and I spent a
number of hours at different times discussing with Kenyatta
the problems of Africa. Cheddi Jagan, when he came over from
the West Indies, recorded a taped discussion with me. He was,
at that time, facing an attempt by the British Government to
re-enter West Indian politics and was concerned by an internal
political struggle he was having with a chap called Burnham,
who subsequently carried the day. He spoke in the City Hall,
and those of us who talked with him were admonished. So we
were able to get the feel of the mind, the power of the mind, the
general integrity of the political leaders who were to become
important figures on the world scene.

And, incidentally of course, when Willy Brandt came to
Britain after the war, it was significant that he came to Newcastle as a result of the efforts of Ernie Popplewell. Again, on a
couple of occasions when he was here, we had an opportunity
to go over many of the European problems with him. He was
one of what I would call the newer generation of social demo-
crats. Somehow we Northerners had managed to bring them
across and get them talking about their problems. This was
because we had a radical tradition and we were also, I think
internationalists. I would consider this to have been an important part of my own political training and experience, and I
hope to some extent of my own political teaching.

Much of this happened in the Socialist Society in Newcastle's
old Royal Arcade. This was a mecca for socialists of all shades
of opinion, no matter where they came from, whether they came
to Britain legally or illegally, and it was not accidental that the

People's Theatre was conceived there, that the Tyneside Film Society was born there, that the Clarion Choir, the Clarion Cycling Club and the Clarion Rambling Club were all spawned in its Victorian caverns. These were movements that were revolutionary in their time and which were born of ordinary people, seeking to pursue the philosophy that those who make films should make them about real things, that life was not concerned only with the glamour of Hollywood, that 'Battleship Potemkin', 'Dr. Caligari's Cabinet', 'Kameradschaft' and 'All Quiet on the Western Front' were the real things. John Osborne is perhaps the most important contemporary analogy in this field. But in the thirties and forties the Royal Arcade culture was looked upon as infantile left-wing illusion. Few people believed that you could write and produce and have people come to see things that were not commercially popular. It was almost like taking the mountain to Mohammed.

I can recall clearly the people who directed my thinking in those turbulent times. Molly Nolan, Billy Beech, Jack Common, and Peggy Murray are some who stand out most vividly and to whom the North owes a debt, and these were ordinary working-class people who, far ahead of their time, appreciated the social function of the arts and the need to find objectives in the pursuit of leisure.

Looking back, it seems almost impossible to believe that when Ghandi came on this scene, bearing in mind his significance in the world, he was treated as the biggest music-hall joke of the thirties and forties. This seemed to me to be so offensive. Here was a man who, whether you agreed with his policy of passive resistance or not, was of tremendous significance. It is salutary to reflect that today such an insult could not be conceived. Television is not all bad. It does create a position where people in spite of themselves put almost anybody on to a pedestal and respect him if he is seen sufficiently. But thirty years ago the picture of the Indian in the minds of too many of our people in Britain was of a fellow trailing a bone, or a Lascar seaman, and they did not recognise that in people like

Ghandi and Nehru we had men who were leading towards a non-violent method of dealing with political questions. Unfortunately Ghandi had no concept of the modern technological society and he therefore trailed in his wake a peasant economy in an age of science and technology.

But who am I to say what they should have been doing? By the middle of the first term of the post-war Labour government it had become obvious that the power of Ghandi, combined with the underlying conviction of Attlee and the Labour movement, made it a certainty that Indian freedom would be granted. Somehow we have a capacity in Britain to claim victories and underestimate the importance of political leaders who spent as much time in Indian prisons and concentration camps as did some of their Western counterparts in fascist countries. Although our Empire did not perhaps sport Buchenwald, conditions in some parts of our overseas territories did not need camps to produce skeletons. They were being produced on the streets of Bombay and Calcutta and in just as emaciated forms as ever came out of Buchenwald. On the one hand, you had these moves towards independence, which were absolutely vital steps forward in the progress of the human race. But because the moves were not understood, I think that the parentage of the colour problem today was, ironically, British. Here we are as a nation, being split down the middle on issues like the South Africans taking part in the Davis Cup and coming here to play cricket. One still has this feeling in the power structure of Britain that the old Empire lives on. We must find a solution to this problem. The beginning of the solution lies in those early efforts of the Indian leaders and the tentative responses of the first Labour government and subsequently in Macmillan, I think, and such Tory leaders as understood what the wind of change in Africa symbolised. Unless we can find the answer to this problem, even though we won the war against the Germans and no matter how we develop atomic weapons, one can see emerging a bigger question even than communism and fascism, but in the same kind of colours—black and white.

So in the late forties it was the impact of Ghandi and Nehru and the fact that the loss of their own liberty had eventually paid off in India, and seemed likely to be repeated in the liberation of other African countries, that began to stimulate me again into more positive thinking and into saying, 'Well, what can I as an individual do about creating conditions, rather than merely protesting?' Because until about 1948 I could have been said to have been the protester; the loudest protester in many cases. I was a rebel and I made myself heard. Back in my boyhood days I used to play a game called 'Relieve-o!' As part of a team of some dozen lads, I would try to avoid capture by a similarly-sized gang. When caught, one was confined in a carefully guarded compound. Eventually only one person was left at liberty. Twelve hunters were in pursuit of him. In the face of such overpowering odds one could still occasionally manage to burst through into the compound, yell 'Relieve-o!' and in one glorious moment release one's pals to fight all over again. This was the sort of crusader I wanted to be in the early post-war days. I did not want to be in the compound. I saw no point in calling 'Scinch' and pleading for clemency in the face of opposition. I wanted to overcome established opposition to personal freedom and to open the floodgates of social opportunity.

4

LOCAL GOVERNMENT

Now how, from being a rebel, did I get into conventiona staid local government? I hadn't given ita thought. One Sunday morning, Arthur Blenkinsop invited me to meet a few friends at his home. He was at that time the M.P. for Newcastle East, and had been closely involved as a junior minister with Nye Bevan in the Health Service. At his home that morning, he had a number of people involved in the Labour Party, and we began to talk about the political situation as it then existed; it was round about five years after the end of the war when the tremendous fervour of the people had begun to disappear. A period of reaction was beginning to set in. The miners were not too sure how far the nationalisation of the mines was going to develop into the wonderful dream that had seemed likely when Shinwell waved his pit lamp. Of course, the nationalisation of the mines had been one of my clarion calls. In the early part of the war, Jimmy Maxton had moved a resolution in Parliament to effect nationalisation, which had been seconded, but attracted only one vote. Now, however, that it had all come about, one could see problems, and we discussed these, together with the Indian dilemma.

Arthur Blenkinsop was particularly interested in the United Nations and the mixed fortunes it was having, the intensification of the cold war, Churchill's Fulton speech and the curtains dropping over Europe. On the home front there was the fact that politics were being reduced to squabbling about rationing, and getting rid of rationing, and whether one wanted more meat or less meat. We knew, of course, that half the people had never had any red meat in any part of their lives anyhow. This was a philosophic retreat from a position that had seemed to promise well for a new post-war society, and our cosy Sunday morning discussion finally centred on this point. Arthur Blenkinsop reminded us that the municipal elections were just round the corner. For the first time, the City of Newcastle had returned a Labour council in 1945 and there was discussion as to what had been achieved by them between '45 and '50. I ventured to suggest that it had been very little. There had been an attempt to build houses of a higher standard against fairly bitter opposition, and old Tom McCutcheon had been in no small measure responsible for this. He actually believed then that there should be two toilets in a house, and although this was only twenty years ago, his heresy was resisted. What we now call higher housing standards were not then considered to be important. Poor Tom McCutcheon's reward was to have named after him on Newcastle's City Road, McCutcheon Court, probably the worst housing development produced anywhere in Britain.

There was almost more human unhappiness caused by Newcastle's post-war housing mistakes than existed in the old pre-war houses. I recall this as a great disservice to McCutcheon. I remember taking the chair when the miserable place was named, and I recall one Labour councillor saying; 'It's a big honour to name these houses after Alderman McCutcheon; to think that little more than two years ago this was nothing but a green field.' And I looked round and saw these awful houses with no grass left. Just mud, greyness and mediocrity. No landscaping and no imagination; and here we were standing on the mud, metaphorically patting ourselves on the back. I thought that McCutcheon's contribution to the city was an important one; he deserved better than that. So did others, namely Hurst, Chapman and Clydesdale.

But to return to the discussion at Arthur Blenkinsop's, I felt that Labour had not really made any notable contribution to our North-East capital. The possibilities had been opened up by Nye Bevan when he made it feasible for local government to contribute in so many new ways to the arts, and prompted those in authority to ensure that education was the rock upon which we built our society. If we went forward with an inadequately educated populace then we could not achieve anything of quality. I could see then, and I can see more clearly now, that whether one has a capitalist society or a communist society or a mixture of both, education is the root upon which American prosperity and Russian prosperity is built. The centres of excellence are clustered around brains, not coal. So far as the North was concerned in 1950, we had to try to get people to understand that it was not just a question of pulling down houses and rebuilding, but of entering into a dialogue on the enrichment of life.

So, as the church bells pealed outside Arthur's house that Sunday morning, I said, 'Yes, I'll have a go. I'll run for Newcastle City Council if the Labour Party will have me.' In saying this, I was conscious of having been a rebel for 20 years, and equally scathing, if not more scathing, in my attacks on the Labour Party than I had been on the Tories. I had been a member of the ILP and, for a brief spell, had become a Trotskyite. I had been expelled from both organisations. I was consistent in being inconsistent, so you can understand that I was not welcomed into the Labour Party with fanfares of trumpets; I went in, looked upon by the older members of the party and some of the younger ones, as a sort of devil incarnate who would not accept party discipline. They were sure that I would do what I wanted to do and say what I wanted to say. They were dead right! I think it was reasonable for them to think so. I was also looked on as a bit of a tub-thumper. I had fifteen years of non-stop soap-box experience; debating with the public, exchanging no-holds-barred views with whoever wanted to listen. The open-air meeting in the thirties and forties was something of importance. I had graduated from the Mound in Edinburgh, and the Bullring in Birmingham, and

Hyde Park Corner, and the Newcastle Bigg Market. Regularly at weekends I would be holding forth at Hedley Street in Wallsend or in the Market Place at Blyth. I had developed some skill, against a largely illiterate background, of using my limited vocabulary to advantage with a crowd, and consequently I not only knew how to start off with a green field with nobody on it, but how to get a crowd, how to build it, and how to hold it; also how to get it thinking and discussing and participating. And this experience ingrained itself in my mind because I knew what communication and togetherness were about. They were about them telling you. You were one and they were many. It was not they who were few and you who mattered. And you could only remain on the platform if you had something to say, because they could walk away, and this was a salutary experience.

So when I joined the Labour Party there were many mutterings from the people who had listened to me uneasily for a decade. In the Labour Party in 1950 there was one person in particular, Ted Corrigan, who had been my persistent heckler down in the Bigg Market. If I saw him I knew I was made; I knew how to provoke him, and if he got provoked, he got worked up, and if anybody got worked up, then the crowd would gather round and enjoy the battle. He was a dedicated defender of everything done by the Labour Party, and a persistent attacker of everything I said. Many years later he was made an Alderman and became one of my best supporters. Whether I had degenerated or he had, I wouldn't know, but the point is that I was applying to be accepted into the Newcastle Labour Party with Ted Corrigan battling away to keep me out, saying, 'He's a Trotskyite; he's an ILP'er; he's been chucked out of both of them, and if they wouldn't have him, why should we?' But I was accepted, and I was nominated for a seat. I had, incidentally, supported the Labour Party in many elections and had worked very hard, because my view was that there was no alternative, so that I did not feel in any way that I had to hang my head in shame, and I didn't believe that I had to agree with

everything that was said. I was asked to appear before the Ward
Party at Walker. I had been helping Arthur Blenkinsop in
Newcastle East, and three or four of us went along to talk to the
committee. This was when my speaking experience helped me.
It was relatively easy for me to take an audience of something
like 50 good Walker folk into my confidence and talk about the
problems that I had been involved in all my life. Walker was a
shipbuilding area. It was, in 1950, an area with a lot of slums,
and I had taken the trouble to do my homework. So I would
talk about Walker as I saw it, and as I would like to see it, and
talk also about the country as I would like to see it, about
Newcastle as I would like to see it, and talk about the world
as I would like to see it. Later we built up a tremendous Labour
Party in Walker, affiliated to the League against Imperialism,
and dedicated to reasoned debate, but in 1950 there was a lot
of petty squabbling.

I was accepted as the candidate by the Walker Party, but
that didn't mean that I was going to be the candidate as far
as the City Labour Party were concerned. There were loud
protests, left, right and centre, but eventually, after plenty of
heated discussion, when I had to stand up to a lot of criticism,
I was successful and fought the seat in Walker. My manifesto,
printed on a shoestring and looking the part, read as follows :

Dear Friends,

I am proud to accept an invitation from a large number
of electors in the Walker Ward to stand as the LABOUR
CANDIDATE at the Municipal Elections on THURSDAY, 11th
May, 1950.

I justly claim to know the needs of the people of
Newcastle, and without possessing any special academic
qualifications, my only desire is to serve in the best
interests of all. As a life-long member of the Trade Union
and Labour Party I have taken a keen interest in all social
problems that effect the lives of our people and my sole
purpose in standing as a Candidate is to help others in
any way I possibly can.

I am deeply conscious of the appalling housing conditions which exist in the City and am far from satisfied that anything of note is being done to alleviate these conditions. If returned as your Municipal representative, I would do all in my power to press for the immediate building of suitable modern flats.

The control of the City Council has been in the hands of the 'Progressives' who have, in addition to their dismal housing record, caused the weekly wage of Car Park Attendants to be reduced from £5 to £4 5s. od. per week, and dispensed with the 5 day week for Corporation manual workers. This is not progress.

If returned as your representative I would consider it my duty to give special attention to the problems which influence the every-day lives of the people—the just claims of the children—the provision of good homes—the care of the aged, the sick and the infirm—an adequate social amenities service and the fostering of a spirit of pride amongst our people.

My purpose is TO SERVE and I trust that with your generous consent the good folks of Walker will return me as their representative on THURSDAY, MAY 11th.

I am, yours sincerely,

D. SMITH

Walker was a traditional Labour seat, so it was no great achievement to win it, but I got quite a good reception from the voters and two important things then followed.

Shortly after the election, the Newcastle Labour Party appointed a new secretary, Joe Eagles, and he was a rare fellow because he had vision and organisational ability. As very often happens in the Labour Party, he was undervalued and never appreciated, but I always admired him because I felt he was a man of principle. The other event, less propitious, was that my election coincided with the loss of power by the Labour Party in Newcastle. I was elected on my birthday, May 11th 1950, and the first Labour group meeting I attended was quite a salutary experience for me. I had seen people losing power before. I had always been a rebel and I had never had anything to do with power apart from getting belted around the ears by it, so I remember going to the first group meeting. Strangely enough, my new colleagues were not discussing what they were going to do tomorrow; they were discussing what they should have done yesterday. I remember one very dear lady, Alderman Mrs. Taylor, saying to me, 'Well, Councillor Smith, if you take my advice you'll serve an apprenticeship. You will listen and say little and then when you've got experience you'll be able to take a more active part in council proceedings.' I was quite flabbergasted. Maybe in 1950 I was a little more big-headed and arrogant than I am now, but I thought, 'Well, good gracious, has this woman lived as long as this and not known all the things that I've been active for in the Labour movement?' Some of the other councillors did know, and therefore the combination of those who wanted to give me help and advice, and those who positively disliked me, made for a difficult situation. I quickly felt disillusioned and was determined to get this out of my system on the day I was introduced to the council. There is a custom at Newcastle whereby the senior councillor for the ward introduces the new member. It is a sort of pale reflection of Parliament. On one's maiden speech one is more or less allowed to say what one wants, therefore no-one ever says anything. But I did not think this was right at all, so I got up and said, 'I'm not interested in platitudes. I've come here to do a job, and I don't feel that the Newcastle City Council has much to be proud of. It is a hundred years since it did anything, and I mean to change that.' Well, that got me off to a bad start. In the city council it was considered a decent thing to say the 'right' thing, but I always felt it was the right thing to say the true thing. I had a clear picture in my mind of the people I was representing because I had talked to them for years. They lived in rotten houses scented by the smells of the Walker bone yard. I was not interested in people dressing up in fancy hats to be the next one on the list for Lord Mayor, pretending they were something that they were not. That is how I felt then and that is how I have felt ever since. I have never lost that feeling. I take the view that perhaps the greatest conceit of all is people who want buildings named after them, or who somehow feel that by a divine right they should allow their name to go forward to be Lord Mayor and that somehow they are then doing a service. Usually, in fact, they just happen to have been around longer than anybody else. The longer you are there, the more people will be defeated or will die and the quicker your turn will come to be Lord Mayor if your party is in power. Thank goodness the system is changing; of course there were good Lord Mayors as well—but few ever fully recovered normality after the experience.

My experience in the field of public speaking naturally stood me in good stead when I went on to the council. At that time the people who were good debaters were undoubtedly skilful. This was particularly so on what was then called the 'Progressive Side'. There were people like Charlton Curry, William Temple and William McKeag. I think Newcastle owes a lot to Temple and Curry in particular. In their different ways they were groping towards the kind of city that they should have been striding towards. But they could not take their colleagues with them. They were split down the middle and down the sides and in almost every direction. But at least they could see what the Town and Country Planning Act could mean. Then there were people like Miss Temple, a gentle, kindly soul, who knew that the money available for the arts was worth spending, and yet could never succeed in getting more than a couple of thousand pounds a year voted. So the council began to be a debating chamber, and every inch of the way was fought.

I continued to feel frustrated, but Joe Eagles would say, 'Now look, you've got to carry on.' If it had not been for him continually cranking me up, I would not have had the guts to battle through the council and through my own group, because it is no secret that I was not only being shot at from the front, but from the back as well. But by good fortune, in the Labour

Party itself, which reflected the trade unions as well as the rank and file and the co-op movement, international issues were beginning to boil up again ; issues such as German rearmament. Clearly, I had an advantage in having been involved in international politics and having talked to international politicians and read practically every philosopher on the issues that mattered to society, so I was able to win through in the City Labour Party, and in 1953 was elected chairman.

I was chairman for three years and could have been for longer if I had not believed that three years is long enough for anybody. But that period was important for me, because leadership was a new thing to me. I believed then, and still believe now, that a leader can only get from his team the best collective wisdom of that team. The only thing that leadership can do is to lift them to greater heights. Or, ultimately, by default, to squander their talents.

The chairmanship of the City Party gave me an opportunity to knit together the organization of Council and Party with the assistance of the executive of the City Labour Party, and Joe Eagles. We set ourselves out to develop the idea that we had been working on in the five years since I had joined the council. We decided for a start, to get our communications right, and we drew up an elementary document called 'Peril in the City', about the slums of Blandford Street and the shocking houses that were being built in their place. For the first time, here was a fully-worked-out, year-by-year plan of how to deal with housing. We could go to people honestly with it and say, 'If we were in power, we could tell you when you would be re-housed. We would be able to give you a choice of a number of places where you could be re-housed.' We introduced, if you like, the first hint of management methods into the debate in the city on the housing programme. We began to talk in architectural terms, in terms of the arts, and in educational terms. We were able to introduce, via the City Labour Party, important resolutions, and get them adopted by the Labour group on the Council. It happened at national level too ; it was by a resolu-

tion of mine at St. Pancras Town Hall that the local government conference of the Labour Party became an annual
conference. It was on a resolution of the City Party that we debated conscription. Then Lord Ted Hill of the boilermakers'
union chose Hepplewhite, and he and I did the first telecast
from a Labour Party conference. At that time, politicians did
not like television and that is how we got in on the act. They
did not like the thought of television cameras intruding into
the inner sanctums of party conferences, but times change
quickly! Once the power of the medium was seen, it soon caught
on. So by using T.V. and the written word, the Labour Party
was pushing out into the region politically. And I was pushing
forward in the Labour group ; pushing ideas forward. And there
was then appearing on the scene in the Labour Party and in the
city council, the raw material, in terms of people, which made it
possible for us to begin to refine the policy upon which, eventually, in 1958, we won power. It was a good victory, against
the political tide at that time. It was only in '59 and '60 that
Labour began to get municipal power in traditionally Tory
areas. When we got power in Newcastle, we could look back
on several out-of-power triumphs.

The first traffic officer in Britain was established on a
minority resolution of the Newcastle Labour Party and it
scraped through by one vote ; that of Arthur Grey, voting
against his own party. The scheme for cleaning up the Tyne was
born in those years in the wilderness, on a resolution of the
Labour Party. The College of Art was successfully debated,
causing a split in the Tories. This was political manoeuvring
if you like, because I was learning fast.

But architecturally, Newcastle was going through the 20th
century dark ages. People ought to undertake penitential
pilgrimages to look at the houses that were built in 1951 in
Benton, and later in Noble Street and Kenton. Many of these
are an indictment of the council which allowed them to be
built, and of the professionals who were prepared to design
them. In these houses you have the prostitution of a profession

by bad political policies. In those days I was intent on discovering how one could get the professionals liberated in order that they could carry out the job that they knew so well without the elected representative somehow destroying their professionalism. This was the germ of the idea which later developed into what I call the new look in local government.

So council meeting followed council meeting. We employed every device, planning carefully as a party and getting things on to the agenda. We really mastered the procedure of that council, and we used every kind of medium for bringing to the attention of people the creative ideas which we wanted to engender. We got power in 1958 decisively, and just as I had been interested to see the 'Fall of the Local Empire' in 1950, so I was interested to see its resurrection. I was, by then, a much more powerful influence in the local Labour group, but still I did not carry the majority with me. However, one Sunday when we discussed tactics in relation to power in the city, I succeeded in persuading my colleagues that we should bring in eight people as aldermen from outside local government, so that we did not have to fight seats, and so that there was the opportunity to pick people who had particular abilities. For it was on ability, imagination, and a sound educational policy that I could see the North advancing.

5

EDUCATION

M<small>Y OWN</small> education was sketchy. I have no chip on my shoulder about that. What I have had always, has been a determination to see that my own children's educational needs were met in the most enriching way. If the state could do this— fine. If not, and if I had money to spend on their schooling, then I would spend it. I consider this to be my right as a parent.

I am an abstemious man, smoking and drinking only modestly, and I have worked only for my family. I have three children. My older daughter went through both the state system and the private system until she qualified as a teacher. My second daughter was privately educated all the time. My teenage son is still at school, and I have paid for him too. If our education system here in Newcastle at the appropriate time had seemed to me to match the needs of my children as individuals, then they would have attended LEA schools. That they did not, meant that I had to exercise my right as a parent, and opt out of the system.

I have been criticised on this count by my left-wing colleagues. 'How,' they have asked, 'could you publicly support comprehensive education, and then refuse to let your own children participate?' The point is facile. I support the building of council houses, but this doesn't mean that I have to live in one. If I want to spend my income, after tax, on education, I still have to pay rates and taxes for other people's children, and I feel no rancour on that score, and no guilt either. We need a new generation of well-balanced individuals. We will get them in different ways. So diversity there must be, but excellence also. Excellence at all levels, and especially in the field of further education.

In the pre-1958 period, the period before Labour got power in Newcastle, the most important debate and the one of most consequence to the city and to the region, was that of the relationship of a modern city to a university and to further education. We did have local people like Charlton Curry, together with a few officers in the corporation who desired to see a university, but I am not sure whether they all had the full educational concept of the need for an independent university as part of the educational structure of the city, and this part of the North, and the relationships between independent universities in Newcastle and Durham and Teesside. I felt that we were missing out badly in the matter of universities in the 50's and 60's, and I feel it more strongly now in the 70's, but the argument of the time was not whether we needed an extension of the University of Durham in Newcastle, but whether we needed an extension at all. Did we need an independent university? The idea had few protagonists. And if we had a university, must it be built around the former Armstrong College, and the Dental College, both city-centre institutions? Could it not be sited outside the city? Many people, including commercial interests, felt that it was a waste of good central area land. So this argument about education and the role of education exposed the real backwardness of the Northern Region at that time, because already one could see in post-war America the prosperity which stemmed from education.

From my point of view, this battle for education was one of the principal fields of activity in the run-up to Labour achieving power. And not only was I convinced that it was essential that Newcastle University become independent, but that colleges of further education should also be in the city centre and should be physically linked to the University. We had Gladys Robson as Chairman of the Education Committee and behind her, pushing very hard, one of the most able of our women councillors, Jessie Scott-Batey.

I described the reaction to this in an interview with Fyffe Robertson on 'Tonight', in September 1962. I had just received the *Architectural Reviews*'s prize as Planner of the Year, and as we looked out over the city, Robertson commented that, in our fight to establish an educational precinct, we were uprooting a whole neighbourhood, and yet the opposition was only sporadic. I told him that we started off from the assumption that people look on planning as something they don't like. They are 'agin it'. It stops them doing things. So we felt that we had to involve people, and make them feel part of the project. We held meetings in church halls and in schools, and they were well attended. We explained our plans to clergymen, the trade unions, business interests and rotary clubs. I personally spoke to over 30,000 people, out of a city of quarter of a million, in three years. Business people wanted to know about the cost, and would it be worthwhile. I had to justify our ideas, and ask them to hold back their own spending for a year or two until our schemes were further advanced. I had to tell householders that their homes were to come down. I handed out pamphlets telling them how to object. They were offered 100% mortgages to purchase new homes and they received market value for their property. And time after time I would hammer home the message that they were having to uproot themselves because educational facilities were needed, not for my children, but for theirs. This was a socially justified exercise. And they responded.

Such opposition as there was rallied behind the banner of Professor Martin Moran. The local papers built him into a hero. He was certainly successful in the short term, resisting attempts by the city to secure sufficient land to integrate further education and university education. I could see two things in this connection. One was that Moran was right to fight to protect the rights of people in affected property. I had it in my mind then that the individual should not suffer for the social good, and this has subsequently influenced my thinking. At the same time I felt that the community was being asked to pay inflated commercial prices for poor residential property. There was a dilemma in my mind; I wanted to reconcile the individual's rights with the social good, and yet not allow the community to be exploited.

Then there were also in my mind judgements to be made on the worthwhileness of an integrated tertiary education complex in the city. How would the students gain? How would Newcastle reap a dividend? The doubts were resolved round a table, in discussions between the city's Director of Education, Mr. Lightfoot, Ted Short, until recently the Secretary for Education and Science, Lord Popplewell who was then M.P. for Newcastle West, Gladys Robson and myself. I threw in a pack of questions : What advantages are there in having colleges far apart and still being called a university? How far can colleges be apart and still get the maximum benefits from further education institutions? Is there a maximum distance, and if so, can we define it? Is it a mile or is it ten miles or is it a yard? Is there not something in fact to be learned from the university campuses that have been established in other parts of the world? This is how the argument went, and eventually, with the exception of one college, we succeeded in winning the locational battle for higher education in Newcastle.

We decided that we wanted all educational institutions located within the city, and we said that we wanted the students to live within a half-mile radius of St. Thomas's church and the Civic Centre. This meant the opening up of qualititive opportunities because of the concentration of students and staff, which would have been impossible had these buildings been spread, as had been the original intention, wherever sites became available and with the appellation of a college of whatever-it-was, or the pretence that it was a university. Of course there were bound to be problems, such as a concentration of students at a certain time of day, and the planning problems that would result from too many people converging on a limited area. But my mind was now clear that with the integration of city and university, and what is now the Polytechnic, and student and businessman and shopper together, there could be all-round enrichment. So ten years ago we won this main argument, and today it is clear that Newcastle has gained from the fact that it has got on the ground the major colleges of the Polytechnic, right in the heart of the city, at the centre of commercial life and at the hub of communications for the whole major subregion.

Furthermore, it has got a close physical link and intellectual association with Newcastle University. Now, we did have in mind further developments, and it is necessary to say where we missed out, and why we missed out. For all that our concept was accepted by the Department of Education and Science, finance flowed from that source into individual colleges and at separate times. It thus became impossible to achieve an integration of heating services, and we could not get an integration for further educational and city library services. It seemed common sense that if the City Library, the University Library and the libraries of the colleges of further education could have been housed in one building, one could have had users who were studying for a Ph.D., or those who, in a humbler capacity, were learning to read and write, rubbing shoulders. Equally could we see in terms of catering, the tremendous potential not only for the students when they were in college, but for the use for conference purposes of the colleges when the students were in recess. If these services had been pooled, Newcastle could have had the basis of a major conference centre. It may still become one. We tried hard to get the integration of dining facilities, but we ended up with separate services in the university, the Civic Centre, the City Library and the colleges of further education. And so they all go merrily on their own way, and one can sense the failure to achieve the qualititive potential combined with efficient practicability because of the methods of allocating capital and reserve finance.

But I must not be churlish about this. I won a lot of skirmishes in this campaign. There were the obvious objections. Why build a library? This was something that could wait for the future. And colleges too. Why not a new office block instead? These arguments betrayed a general lack of appreciation of the educational deficiencies of the North East. Even from one's nominal allies there was the demand for the quick-build rather than the planning and integration of ideas, of buildings and of people's needs, and people's environment, which we saw as a long, slow process. So we found ourselves having to fight actions on several fronts, and sometimes we lost. The People's Theatre moved into the suburbs at Heaton. If ever a building, an institution, a group of dedicated artists should have been integrated into the city's education precinct, it was the People's Theatre. Yet here we had this progressive group opting out of the city centre; not prepared to wait a year or two, in order to achieve something of major significance. The stimulation which we were injecting into the arts by our thinking, was not accepted by the city's finest amateur group. We had a similar sort of battle with the Stone Art Gallery, which rightly fought for its prosperity, and in so doing did much to stimulate interest in the arts and local culture. It was then that I first met Norman Cornish.

It was interesting to me that those people whom one could have expected to rally to the bigger idea, while often in the vanguard, seemed to be fighting against those of us who were really fighting the same battle as them. So we missed out on several issues. But there were other clouds on the horizon.

When the Labour group got into power, it ran straight into the storm of comprehensive education; battle was joined very bitterly here. We had two resignations immediately we tabled our ideas on comprehensive education. City-University relations were strained. The situation in general in many Newcastle schools was deplorable. The schools by the river were dreadful. Cruddas Park, West Walker, and East Walker schools contained kids who were almost doomed to failure. We could build ships, but we couldn't launch human beings. One had only to look at the records and realise that this could not continue. I myself did not claim to know much about the pros and cons of comprehensive education, but overall I could see that the existing system was producing the wrong kind of answers. Our universities and colleges of further education required a judicious blend of students from outside the region and inside the region; this mixture of students could be achieved as a result of the activities we were stimulating. But I could not see them developing in a balanced way because of the small percentage of children coming out of our city schools and going on to further education. So I was converted to comprehensive education, while at the same time being concerned that this transition should be handled as sensibly and humanely as possible. I spent a lot of time talking to the head of Rutherford College, Roger Bennett, who was a personal friend of mine, and to the head of the Grammar School. Professor Tuck and the Vice-Chancellor of the University of Newcastle resigned from the city's education committee, and I considered this to be playing at politics in a surprising and disappointing way. I did not hesitate to say so.

All of this was hard work. Persuading, cajoling and jollying-along people became my stock in trade. But that was the only way I could do it. I am not a hard man. In no sense am I ruthless. But I am determined. Once having made up my mind, I dig my heels in and will not give up easily. By this time I was in my 40's and the Richardson Dees School was a long way behind me. But I was conscious that a whole new generation of youngsters was passing through that school, and hundreds like it on Tyneside. I wanted them to have every chance of developing their talents to the full. If my persuasion sessions with the people of Newcastle could help any of those kids to a fuller life, then my late nights and sore throats were worth it.

6

LET'S BUILD A CITY

NEWCASTLE is a fine city. When one looks at the wonderful buildings still standing after 136 years—buildings that formed part of the John Dobson major central area development scheme—it is hard to realise that at the time they were being erected working men were engaged for six days a week for a daily wage as low as 4/- for carpenters, 4/6 for stonemasons and 1/8 for day labourers. And they were returning to homes which contained no amenities at all, not even water in the house. A compensating factor, admittedly, was that rum and brandy were sold for as little as 3/- a gallon! The low standard of housebuilding was not because of the impossibility of producing the right kind of house, but because the right kind of house was not then considered necessary. My feeling has always been that we must look sufficiently far ahead to ensure that an increasingly high standard of living and an ever-increasing amount of leisure are catered for by buildings which, though they may appear to have uses in advance of their time, will be adequate for the requirements of tomorrow. So in Newcastle I wanted to see the creation of a 20th century equivalent of Dobson's masterpiece, and its integration into the historic framework of the city. If this could be achieved, I felt, then our regional capital would become the outstanding provincial city in the country. The method of development, as I saw it, was to make good existing deficiencies by a new central area redevelopment. This development, to be successful, had to have broad public support, and this would be achieved by the same sort of dialogue that was being carried on in connection with the education precinct. It was essential also to have a co-ordinated team of developers, working with each other and with the local authority. This would ensure that the sculptor and the landscape architect would be accepted as part of the development pattern. Just as people go to Princes Street in Edinburgh—the next main street north of Newcastle— merely to stand and stare, so I wished them to be attracted to the centre of Newcastle for purposes other than shopping. I wanted the pedestrian to remain supreme in the shopping areas, while the motorist had to be given adequate provision. I have never been a traffic Canute—the modern city needs as much traffic as possible, and must deal with tomorrow's traffic problems today. I was determined that Newcastle would not accept just any architect whom the developer might wish to impose on it. I felt it wrong that when a city was beginning to take care to ensure that its public buildings were of the highest standard and best design, it should show less concern about its central redevelopment. The best of our national and international architects were to be commissioned. So too with building organizations. They had to be the most reliable and reputable. It was important, too, that they should attract young apprentices, so that their craftsmanship might be developed and their imaginations fired by the exciting project.

So there I was in 1958, with a vision of a city. But what else did I have? Well, I had eight years of council service behind me, I had learnt a little about tactics, and rather more about political infighting. I had also secured a good ally and learned counsel in Professor Joe Allen. He was in charge of the country's first Department of Town and Country Planning, at the University of Newcastle. He had a tremendous sympathy for people, and we took to each other from the beginning. We had long discussions on the place of people in planning, and the relationship between the economist and the planner, and the thorny problem of the elected representative's responsibility to the

professional planner. Professor Allen was a behind-the-scenes
worker, who did much to advance my thinking, and even more
to help the city of Newcastle. His contribution to the establishment of the City Planning Department, a prototype for the
country, under Wilfred Burns, was considerable. But he never
received the credit which was due to him. He was a pioneer with
kid gloves ; a prophet in an urban wilderness.

Did I have any other allies? Well, I was proposed as the leader
of the city Labour Party in 1958, and I netted 14 out of a
potential 60 votes. So that was my backing at the time. Earlier,
when I was elected deputy-leader, my enemies ensured that
two deputy-leaders were appointed. I was far from being the
blue-eyed boy of the left. My enemies were legion. They just
did not trust me, nor did they understand me. I talked a
different language. My arguments were about inner cabinets in
local government, efficiency as a complement to caring, and
planning as the handmaiden of a civilized life. Their talk was
of drains and majorities and rates. These were important things,
but not priorities in a city which was being strangled by traffic,
humiliated by lack of opportunity and murdered by mediocrity.

I had some ammunition however, of an unlikely kind. This
was the inept scheme of our so-called 'Progressive' predecessors ;
a 20th century entrance to Newcastle. It was at the south end
of Pilgrim Street, where the A1 trunk road strode proudly
north over the Tyne Bridge, and then faltered as it entered the
car-choked city. From the east coast, City Road added its quota
of diesel fumes, while heavy vehicles from Carlisle in the west
contributed to the confusion. Edinburgh threw its battalions
southwards with as great enthusiasm as it had ever mustered
in border frays. But with less success, for Pilgrim Street humbled
everything and everyone. Jags and Daimlers alike were cut
down to size. Pedestrians grew old while waiting to cross the
road. Office workers received ear plugs with their coffee.

The Progressive solution to this mountainous problem was
a mouse of a roundabout. Before we took power, they had
succeeded in getting their plans approved by Whitehall.

Through the influence of Professor Allen I was introduced to the chief planner in the Ministry of Housing, Professor J. R. James, now of Sheffield University. I discussed with him at some length the tragedy that the proposed Pilgrim Street roundabout would be as a gateway to Newcastle. Already I felt that Gateshead on the opposite side of the Tyne had missed great opportunities in its integrated planning of the A1 artery. The bridge which it had conceived was a really miserable example of engineering and design and unless we could make sure that in widening out the entrance to Newcastle, we had a scheme which matched the challenge of the times, then we could not build a great city. We could not succeed in making any headway unless we stopped the existing Pilgrim Street roundabout scheme in its tracks. Well, this was rather new in local government. The city officers of the time, may have thought, I suppose, 'Good God, you must spend the money when you've got it; you never spurn money. Any island is better than no island at all.' To further complicate the issue, a principle of preservation was involved. In the immediate area were the Holy Jesus Hospital and the Royal Arcade, both part of Newcastle's heritage. So we had engineering and architectural dilemmas; we had preservation and new construction as uneasy bedmates; we had a multitude of arguments to go through and battles to fight in a small area. The interesting thing then was that the first major battle within our Labour group was concerned with stopping something; it was a battle to stop spending. It was an attack on deplorable design and inadequate reasoning. It was a condemnation of the Progressive plan to destroy ancient buildings without regard for their true value.

Together with my small band of supporters, I fought this battle bitterly through the Labour group. There is no doubt that some of the people involved saw the whole thing in terms of intense hostility towards me. But I had with me colleagues like Lady Wynne-Jones, Nobby Bell, Ted Fletcher, Bob Brown, and many others. We liked to think that we were truly dedicated

to building a great city. We won the battle in our group. Then
we began to find that other people who had been quite happy
to accept the barren, desolate island without a squeak, began to
take an interest. Included in these were the Northern Architectural Association and the Northumberland and Newcastle
Society, both of which, it seemed to me, had acquiesced in the
former concept of a city's desecration, but which now expended
great zeal in trying to stop our more enlightened plans. So we
had to engage in a series of discussions which I felt was good
and right, but which invariably involved me saying, 'Why the
hell do you always argue with us? Why don't you come forward
positively and in defence of things rather than react against
them?' And now again in the 70's, many of the same people are
crying woe about proposals to remodel Newcastle's Central
Station. Why did they not buckle on their aesthetic armour
fifteen or twenty years ago when it was suggested to them?

However, in 1958 we had a lot of wrangling to undertake on
preservation. We listed all the buildings and all the areas that
we wanted to preserve. We also faced the fact that we might not
agree on the way we wanted them safeguarded for posterity.
An example of this occurs in a quiet oasis at the bottom of Bath
Lane in Newcastle. There, under the city walls, cradled by
soothing lawns, you have a place to dream in. Yet around its
edges are railings which perpetuate the worst design of the
thirties. The historic significance of the area stands affronted.
One can get preservation which is nice and cosy, but we wanted
preservation that was more genuine. We felt that if we did not
appreciate the rare quality of what we were preserving, we
could not create something new that was going to match the
best of the old. As we used to say in debates, do we always have
to go Athens to see the Acropolis? We are going to build our
own new buildings which people are going to come here and
admire. So we fought and won the battle for Holy Jesus; we
fought and won the battle for the preservation of the Royal
Arcade, albeit in a pseudo sense. But if you see it today, incorporated in the new Swan House, you may agree that it was

a battle worth fighting. And when the skirmishing was over, it meant that we could have a multi-level city; we could take the traffic out of the city, and fashion a ring around the inner city. In a sense we were creating a modern city wall. When Newcastle was finished, one would be able to come under gateways at Pilgrim Street and the Great North Road, Claremont Road and the West Road. This is how it was conceived. Every major entrance to Newcastle was to provide the sense of coming into a modern enclosed city. Once it is completed, this is what will happen. It will be possible within this redeveloped centre, for pedestrians to wander from offices to shops, to university, to library, to civic centre, and to have an active, alive community, able to walk and talk and dally without the threat of being run over.

Following our victory on the Pilgrim Street roundabout, we were able to welcome Derek Bradshaw as our new City Engineer into a city of increasing vision. He was a person with whom I found it easy to work and I am quite certain that the new Redheugh Bridge, designed as it is by good architects and engineers, will make its contribution to the tradition of the North for civil engineering.

Other engineering works in the city have all benefited from this discussion about design, and reflect an appreciation for detail, recently non-existent in the North. This already applies to the bridge completed over the end of the Tyne Bridge. It will apply to the one over City Road. It applies in particular to Swan House, that soaring companion to the Pilgrim Street roundabout.

A chap once came to me and said, 'Why is it that the North never honours the people who have contributed to its prosperity? Swan made some of the most remarkable discoveries of the early industrial revolution, including the filament in the electric bulb, and artificial silk.' I said, 'Right, that's an aspect we've never thought about. What do we do?' and he said, 'I don't know, but I think we should do something.' I asked if any of the family were alive, and he said, 'Yes, there's Sir

Kenneth Swan.' So I went to London to meet Kenneth Swan.
He must have been about 80, a man of superb mind and what
I would imagine, had I known Bertrand Russell at all, that
gentleman would have been like. We talked over the matter.
But at the end of it all, he said, 'What I would like to see in
Newcastle is a swan, frozen in full flight. I think this would be
a tribute to my father.' My response was, 'I'm going to throw
something into this argument. Why not a fountain illuminated
by changing lights and a piece of modern sculpture depicting
the element in the light bulb together with artificial silk?'
Kenneth Swan was aghast. I said, 'Now, look, if your father
represented anything, he represented a break with yesterday
and I'm quite certain he wouldn't have wanted a swan. It's so
corny. It's not worthy of him, and it's certainly not worthy of
you.' So eventually he was won over to my idea and we set up
a committee which included Bob Clough of Thomson Press.
We did a lot of lobbying and eventually had our plan approved.
Sir Kenneth, the last survivor of Sir Joseph's eight children
came to perform the unveiling of the visual analogy, the work
of Raymond Arnott, and this made it all worthwhile. He was
by then 94 years young and spoke without notes. His remarks
were lively and pertinent, and I was flattered when he made a
passing reference to the fact that the idea had been born and
developed during our discussions in London. Not only was
Swan House, and the Pilgrim Street roundabout, an argument
about what should be preserved and what should not be
preserved, it was additionally an opportunity to put on the
ground an example of what those of us who were pursuing this
argument were trying to create. So it had to be good architecture; it had to be good planning; it had to have this 'city wall'
feeling about it; it had to be of materials that belonged to the
area; it had to be strong because it was up against the railway
and in the centre of a mass of traffic. Its scale had to be right
because it nudged the Holy Jesus Hospital. And it had to con-
tain the Royal Arcade as well as symbolise the achievements of
Joseph Swan. By this time we were able to discuss in the city

debating chamber the kind of city that we wanted. Not just simply saying, 'Well, let's rebuild it.' Now we were able to say, 'If architect A is to work beside Architect B or C, or if A is in the middle of B or C, or C's in the middle of A and B, what kind of city do we create?' We could see that it was necessary for us to have policies not only for the preservation of old buildings, but for the heights of new buildings and for the materials that were to be used in new buildings, and that was where one became involved in commercial arguments, say with Littlewoods or the British Home Stores or Marks & Spencers. We could not expect them automatically to use local stone. Where it was to be used, we were arguing for stone from quarries like Springwell or Blaxter, and Portland stone was writ large on most of their plans. We knew we could never persuade these commercial stores to use our stone; it was a costly business for them to develop in the city centre. So we had to reach a compromise. Basically, what we felt was that the character of the city could be best expressed in either black or white; evidence of this is now to be seen in Marks & Spencers which has aggregate panels largely white; Littlewoods Stores is mainly black. This theme will, when the city areas are finished, be seen to make sense. The point is that we were not content to say to these people : 'Build your Marks and Spencers store here as you build it in every other city.' We cared enough to bargain with them and to have arguments with them. I remember particularly having a public argument with the Barclays Bank people about a site they wanted to develop in Northumberland Street. It was one of the most difficult cases I ever had to make, because I could see their lawyers sitting in the public gallery, and not only had I to be careful what I said, but I had to be able to stand up if necessary in a public enquiry and defend the line we were taking. What I was saying was that if this one building was allowed to be developed before we had worked out plans for the services under the ground, and the level of the pedestrian access above the ground, then we would have to build the city around Barclays Bank. We won the argument, but in a sense we lost a battle. We were allowed time to develop our case, which we did, and we were allowed to develop our plans, which we did, and we got the planning concept right. Barclays were adequately compensated for anything that they had lost by the planning refusals that they had been forced to accept. On reflection, I am sure they appreciated our views.

There was a somewhat similar case in nearby Grey Street, that superb testimony to Dobson, which I was determined to keep sacrosanct. The Midland Bank wanted to insert a piece of modern architecture, and I felt that this would be the end of the street. So I stuck my neck out and said 'No.' I was accused of carrying a torch for ersatz Dobson, but the Planning Committee supported me, and I am prepared to be judged by the completed building. In all of these continuing arguments one sensed a lifting of the sights of both councillors and officers.

As our eyes wandered over the city, and as we patiently, yet doggedly pushed on with our five year plan, we were gradually evolving new ways to get things done. Our local M.P.s were asked to clear the lines with successive housing ministers, and our councillors and officers built bridges to the civil servants in Whitehall. We took short cuts around beaurocratic obstacles and I caused raised eyebrows when I hired a Rapide aircraft to make flying visits to see candidates for our important new appointment of a Planning Officer. Young architects became excited, and began to produce pictures of what Newcastle could look like. Our first big city plan got the front page story over the Russian astronauts' first space flight. Long live the editor of the *Evening Chronicle*! Press and television, albeit a little reluctantly, were sensing that local government had moved from the parish pump era into the big business league. After all, the cost of our new city had been estimated at some £200 million. One could not afford to process ratepayers' contributions of that dimension through the tortuous procedures of Victorian-type committees. And one could not, either, settle for other than the best in conceiving what was being referred to as the New

Brasilia. This was why, when we turned our attention to city-centre Eldon Square, we aimed for the sky.

Eldon Square was one of the few squares in Newcastle. Few of these exist in any of our Tyneside towns. And rightly, people said, 'It's too good to knock down. It's precious. Leave it alone.' But no-one ever looked at the back of Eldon Square. It was a ghastly sight; the old joke about Queen Anne front and Mary Ann back applied to Eldon Square. And, equally symbolic, the only nearby building that had been erected in the 30 years from 1930 to 1960 was a hefty labour exchange in Prudhoe Street. So on the one hand you had this huge labour exchange, and on the other you had the impressive elevation of Eldon Square and the pleasant leisure area in front of it. I was convinced that there was only one architect who could replace Eldon Square with something that could be better in the 20th century tradition. Or rather, I had it in mind that there was a possible combination of two architects, one developing Eldon Square and one developing the nearby Green Market area. The two I had in mind were Arne Jacobsen and Le Corbusier. But I did not say anything to anybody at that stage because I realised that our local architects were bellyaching already about us bringing in Basil Spence and Robert Matthews. It did not matter if Woolworth's brought in their own architect; they could bring in whom they liked, but if we imported outsiders, it did matter. My colleagues and I were, in fact, feeling our way towards the concept of an architectural trio for our new city. The trio was to consist of Arne Jacobsen, Basil Spence and Robert Matthews. With them, I felt, not only could we bring to fruition the university-education precinct idea, but we could talk of physically linking our buildings above ground level, so that one could have students moving above their colleges as well as through them.

Gradually from 1958, this idea took shape. It was necessary, because up to then architectural and planning decisions in our university too often reflected the worst of the past. The Physics Block was one of the few good exceptions that had been built

just after the war. So we had an architects' battle on our hands
with the university too. Well, ideas are fine, but I have always
been a person for doing things, so I said to my wife that we had
to persuade Arne Jacobsen to come here. Quite frankly, if we
had invited him to Newcastle, I do not know how we could
have kept him. Apart from Dobson's work, he would have seen
nothing to inspire him. So off Ada and I went to London, to the
Danish Embassy. I met the ambassador and reminded him that
the links between Denmark and Newcastle were strong. How
pleasant it would be to foster the relationship between the North
of England and the Scandinavian countries. And then I came
to the point. I wanted, if possible, to get Arne Jacobsen into
Newcastle. I also talked to Alan Bullock at St. Catherine's
at Oxford, because Jacobsen had worked on that college and
integrated it sympathetically, I thought, into the surrounding
town and countryside, keeping it beautifully below tree-level.
It created no problems in that interesting city. He said, 'Right,
I'll have a word with him and then you can follow it up.' I
did follow it up.

My wife and I set off for Scandinavia on our own initiative,
without asking the city to sponsor us or bless our visitation.
We went off on a pilgrimage to speak with Arne Jacobsen and
to look at some of his ideas in housing and city-centre work.
We spent much time looking at his split-level houses, and some
of his school work which was equally famous. We admired his
break-down of large school units into intimate courtyards so that
the group in the school was small, even if the school was large. To
Jacobsen the individual matters. We envied his hotel development. Ten years ago there were few hotels in Newcastle and
you could not get a meal after about 9 o'clock at night. And so
we spent a good deal of time looking over a newly-completed
hotel in Copenhagen. It had been built for SAS, the Scandinavian Air Service. The architecture was superb. There were
problems in terms of cost and operational efficiency, but I came
away convinced that our man would come over here and have
a look round, and that we could get him. And, of course, we did,

after he had been fed into the council machinery. He was a valuable member of our multi-pronged assault on architecture.

Now, remembering up to that stage that the modern buildings in Newcastle had not been of an illustrious character, it was perhaps surprising to find opposition to bringing a foreigner to work in Newcastle. What I felt was that Jacobsen decided to take on this commission, as opposed to a number of others which he had been offered in India, Pakistan, Australia and Canada, because he recognized a combination of dedication and flexibility in our approach to planning. It gave us the strength we needed to press ahead with the demolition of Eldon Square; it is to the credit of Arthur Grey and the group currently in power in Newcastle that they have not destroyed the Jacobsen concept. They have whittled away some of it, but when built, it is what I would consider to be one of the North's most dramatic new buildings, and I cannot think that there will be another like it in the next decade or even in the 80's or 90's which will be as striking as this tall, pencil-slim, aluminium-clad block which will stand in Eldon Square by 1975. And this, of course, provides an example of the time scale in which planners work. Jacobsen was saying 'yes' in 1960. It will be 1975 before his building is complete. And I wonder how many people know what his building will look like? I should think one could count them on four hands. This is bad. I suppose that I had the vision, and I like to imagine it finished. So often people do not live long enough to see a vision become reality. But in 1960 I could stand back, take a deep breath, and feel that things were getting done.

Burns had been appointed late in 1960 and his brief was clear. We were consulting with people to an extent which was being looked upon as an interesting political phenomenon. For the first time, I could detect that the professional was being thrust forward under my verbal admonition that the kind of city I want cannot be built by the kind of man I am. This meant that professionals were now prepared to come and work in Newcastle because they knew that the popular picture of me being a dictator and directing everything that went on was false. When they worked here, they had a great deal of freedom and plenty of creative opportunity within the framework of an enlightened policy. The press played an interesting part in this. When Burns came here, we gave him six months to prepare his first plans on the basis of the policy we had laid down in principle. For some reason, the press felt it necessary to build Wilf Burns into a kind of opposition candidate to myself. Now, I never resented this ; it never troubled me at all. But I have always thought that Burns could have been more generous to his professional colleagues who worked with him, and without whom we could never have succeeded. He could well have afforded to indicate that the re-building of Newcastle was not a one-man band, or a one-profession band. This is the clear definition of the role of the professional vis à vis the elected representative. This is what makes things possible. Unless you get this relationship right and you define the areas of responsibility correctly, you cannot succeed.

But we did succeed. One of the most remarkable and tangible results was the tremendous increase in land values in the city. Unfortunately, a city cannot directly cash in on these. It has no direct equity capital. If it had, it would be possible to let people live in Newcastle almost rent-free because of the tremendous increases in value that were created by that decade-old initiative of the city. The present, in other words, benefits from the activities of the past, the future from today's. This is, as I see it, crucial. Whether it is in the arts, education, commercial development or whatever, the real benefits flow to tomorrow's citizens. That is why there is no doubt in my mind that the 'canny toon' will be the city of the future.

D.C.L. *Honoris Causa*

(*Newcastle Chronicle and Journal*)

With Harold Wilson

(*Northern Echo*)

(*Cartoon by courtesy of Gerald Scarfe and the Sunday Times*)

With Hugh Gaitskell

(*Newcastle Chronicle and Journal*)

Chairman of the Northern Economic Planning Council
with his personal copy of *Challenge of the Changing North*
(Central Office of Information; Crown Copyright)

With Dennis Howell, Lord Lonsdale and Walter Winterbottom
(Northern Echo)

7

GANNIN' ALANG THE SCOTSWOOD ROAD

THE YEAR is 1958. It is 11 p.m., dark and cold, with an October chill prompting the thought that the North-East winter is waiting in the wings. A man never feels his best at such times, and I am no exception. Trudging home through New-castle's streets, from the Old Town Hall in the Bigg Market, up through the Haymarket and past the Royal Victoria Infirmary, I ponder on the worthwhileness of it all. The council meetings that go on and on. The committees which suffer from procedural strangulation. And Noble Street—my goodness, Noble Street! This was the greatest architectural and human disaster ever inflicted on Newcastle. And it was not a relic of the Industrial Revolution, but a contemporary housing development. The Noble Street flats were an indictment of civic misguidedness. They provided the kind of environment which militated against a happy family life. I used to haunt them and talk to the residents. They were so miserable and degraded by their homes that I was masochistically drawn to them. Everything was a mess.

And here I am walking home after an afternoon at Noble Street and a whole night wrangling about costs and rates and drains. I turn into Belle Grove Terrace; the lights are going out in the public house at the end. People have been having a good time there while I have been sweating it out over estimates—figures that are really symbols for human happiness and family fulfilment. There is something wrong with the system. Or maybe it's me. Perhaps I should forget it all and go and play golf. The temptation to opt out is strong.

c

Belle Grove Terrace is old, solid and dependable. Three storeys tall, with basement rooms, it sits prim and Victorian, with its moorland apron spread out before it. I turn into number 13. The clang of the iron gate is a stimulus that evokes thoughts of warmth and coffee and slippered indulgence. I climb the stone steps to the front door. And then I think of two of my labour colleagues and the dig they took at me earlier in the evening : 'Why should you make such a fuss about houses ? You live in Millionaires' Row. You're all right!' And my testy rejoinder : 'I paid £600 for my house. And I'll swap my money for yours any day.' The front door opens, and the warmth, the light and the smell of food envelop me. But it is not good. The spell is broken. I am in a black mood, and my family must make the best they can of me. And so they do, just as they always have done, and, I trust, always will.

It is impossible for me to remain unaffected by human unhappiness. I have to hit out at someone. Can I start, in the case of houses, with architects? Why are they not more self-critical? Should they not have been the first people to show a sensitive awareness of the Noble Street disaster? And should they be content to see awards being given to members of their own profession for designing outstanding single buildings regardless of the fact that much of their work is mediocre, and their contribution to society undistinguished? If a building looks all right, even though the price is wrong and the quality of thinking behind it is poor, should this merit an award? I tried to clarify these points with members of the Northern Architectural Association, but without success. When I left the Newcastle Council, although I had been chairman of the housing committee, I felt disappointed about the city's housing record. I still maintain that if one is to get the sort of homes which will meet the needs of people moving from slum areas, there is a necessity for architects to be exposed to a training different from that provided currently in schools of architecture. As an antidote to the poverty of ideas in 1958, I tried hard to introduce artists as catalysts in the creation of our urban houses and landscapes.

Professor Rowntree of the Fine Arts Department of the University of Newcastle collaborated with me in this ploy. But it came to nothing. The mystique of professionalism won the day. And the opportunity to make something exciting of the spectacular topography of Newcastle, with its sweep southwards to the river, was lost. I recall seeing Pasmore working with an architectural team at the new town of Peterlee in County Durham. To watch his houses develop was to immerse oneself in visual poetry. A second chance for Newcastle lies in the rebuilding of Byker, the east end sprawl of closely-packed terraces crouching over the Tyne. Erskine's approach to this challenge is encouraging. His work may well match the marvellous spirit of the people he is serving. For serving them he is, and this goes for all of us who at any time have the privilege of providing houses for the people.

When the Labour group took power in the city in 1958, I think we could claim to have produced the first adequately-thought-out housing programme in Britain. It had refinements. We dealt with the problem of eviction and it was to me a proud boast that those people on our council, particularly Connie Lewcock, who were responsible for welfare and eviction could claim that after we had been in power about three years, no-one was on the streets of Newcastle through eviction. There was no other city which could say that. We had worked this out and it was of sufficient importance for a lot of areas in Britain to benefit from our thinking. However, the first thing that we did when we came to power, and I became chairman of the housing committee, was to go into the architects' department and say, 'Right, no more Noble Streets. These are out.' We had to compromise between virtually stopping the housing programme to give us time to work out new designs, and making the best of the designs that existed. We had a critical situation on our hands, with a waiting list of nearly 10,000 families, and not an acre of building land in the city boundaries. So the first thing we had to do was to persuade Whitehall to recognize the urgency of the land problem; Mr. Henry Brooke who was housing minister at the time has to his credit the fact that he responded. I have always had a soft spot for him because he never seemed to get the credit for anything he did in any ministerial job. I found him a person who had a great deal of sympathy for people. Perhaps it was his brittle kind of voice which made him unpopular. Ted Short, who was M.P. for the Scotswood Road area was a tremendous help to us, and we worked out and agreed with Whitehall, a five year programme. With the co-operation between civil service and our own staff we succeeded in getting a clearance order through in record time. We were lucky that there were no objectors or we would have had to have public enquiries and all sorts of delays. As things were, we found it possible to get weaving on what was called the Scotswood Road Development, and the fact that we were able to do this within six months of achieving power had a dramatic effect. We had to use multi-storey blocks that had been on the stocks for years and had not been built, but we were able to create around them the concept of open space. With discreet floodlighting we were able to carry the greenness of the lawns and the dappled shadows of the trees into the North-East night. They were well-fitted, good flats, they were a credit to their designers, and they were low in cost.

This was a difficult time in my life. My wife was very ill and I remember sitting down and writing a ream of poetry about Scotswood Road, which I had known since boyhood, and how it was changing. I imagine that it is only a Tynesider who can wax nostalgic about this throbbing, grimy, lovable, ugly artery. Shades of Coffy Johnny and Cushy Butterfield rip-roar their way along it to the long-gone Blaydon Races. And now the road was being reborn. It was, in a way, so symbolic, so romantic, that I could not help but write about it :

> 'From Cruddas Park on to Rye Hill
> We are determined, have the will
> That horrid slums we shall erase
> With surgeon's knife and then replace.
> Proud still stands St. Stephen's spire

Looking down on watchman's fire
As all around now disappears,
The church still stands—it sheds no tears—
And says 'Goodbye' to row on row
Of houses now all doomed to go.
It preens itself—must look alive
For people who will soon arrive.
Banks on which did children play,
Old folk climbed their weary way,
Out of breath as up they went
On daily round or task then bent.
The banks today are still and gaunt,
And ghosts of yesterday now haunt
The site, part empty, standing cleared
Where demolition's sword has seared.
Still remaining, coping stone—
Painted, shining, all alone
Among the others, drab and grey
All will soon be hauled away.
Here and there among the rubble,
Quite apart from seeming trouble
Stands a privet hedge, aloof,
Glancing upward to the roof—
A roof now part devoid of slate
Apprehensive of its fate;
A roof no longer catching rain
(From criticism please refrain).
No. 40 swinging wide,
A rotten floor it used to hide.
There, yesterday, the neighbours chattered
Of things that really little mattered.
Deserted cat gives plaintive wail—
Stops awhile to lick its tail—
Gazes round without a friend,
'Can this really be my end?'
Gardens tended with such care

Now provide a sight so rare
A small grass patch, just like a jewel—
Timbers carted off for fuel;
Chimney stack still standing gaunt—
Wisps of far-off smoke now taunt.
Where are you, slums of yesterday?
Your changing face, now sad, soon gay.
Here and there a gable wall
Exposing papers to us all—
Flowered, plain, in stripe or check
Silent parchments watch men wreck
As building after building falls
Leaving exposed these few odd walls;
Wherein once sheltered windows clean,
Now only broken glass is seen.
Flats soon reaching for the sky—
Future tenants question why
It should be them through Heaven sent
(Maybe they can't afford the rent)
Will the piano go through the door?
Hear the neighbour through the floor.
What will you do with that noisy one?
If they're to stay, then we'll be gone.
Where can we let the children play?
When it's our turn will we have a 'say'
In the Estate where we'll have to live?
Or must we accept what the Council give?
Old Scotswood Road must live again
To carry further still its fame.
We're soon to have a celebration—
Let Tyneside rise in jubilation.
A century has marched along
Since first we heard that Tyneside song.
On June the 9th in '62
We will tell the world anew—
Together with the sculptor's art,

A Festival to play its part.
We'll make Tyneside thus loud proclaim
How just and right its shout of fame—
Tomorrow, then, we all will see
That Scotswood's making history.'

And on 9th June 1962 there was indeed a recreation of the
Blaydon Races, with carriages leaving Balmbra's Music Hall
in Newcastle and jog-trotting their way westwards along the
famous old route. How Hugh Gaitskell enjoyed that day. But
the 4-year housing slog which preceded this event was a trying
period. With no land available, what could we do but close our
waiting list of applicants for council houses, and get on with the
job of clearing the Scotswood Road slums? It was not a popular
decision. It meant an argument within the Labour group before
we could close the list. The narrow majority in favour of the
idea was only secured on the basis of our officers being able to
promise a quarterly progress report on the clearance work, so
that the waiting list could be reopened at the earliest moment.
And as a lot of people on the waiting list lived in slum houses in
any case, we were able to have full public participation in the
housing programme. We embarked upon a series of meetings
throughout every part of the city, and these meetings were
packed to the doors. I think I could claim that they were the
prototypes of Skeffington Report-type consultations, although
Wilf Burns had experience in Coventry of similar situations.
Coventry were certainly pioneers, but theirs was a relatively
small city expanding, whereas ours was a large city contracting
in terms of housing. Our meetings were remarkably successful.
They were not easy meetings, because we were really bringing
bad tidings of no joy to so many people; there were very few
people who were being told that they were going to get a house
next week; some of the people were being told that they would
not have a house for ten years. But the interesting thing was
that once the people knew where they stood, they were at least
more content. What was difficult was to get across to one's
political colleagues that it was sometimes better to tell the

truth than to compromise and pretend that in compromising you would achieve anything. I think it would be fair to say that our reason for keeping power in the city for nine years (and I still think that it could have been twelve years) was because we never pretended that one could get anything for nothing. We knew that the city would cost money; what we were saying was: 'Sacrifice collectively for your children as you would individually', and we found that people responded to this plea at the polls in '58, '61 and '64. We won these elections by holding difficult seats and consolidating our position despite a tremendous controversy always taking place around the group and around me in particular. To the ordinary man in the street I was in some ways looked upon as a saint, yet to many of my own colleagues, and certainly my opponents, I was the devil incarnate. I never fully understood why this was so. I suspect that it may have been because I was still a fighter for fine things at a time when the popular cry was for more and more, however shoddy the product. And again there was the strange communication gap. I did not think it enough to talk about four rooms, kitchenette, bathroom, and windows that opened outwards. I just had to employ imagery which set houses against a pastoral background.

I used to try to get this across to my colleagues by asking them what it was they liked about the Lake District. 'Why do you like water and mountains?' I would query. 'Think about it, talk about it. Why is it that when buildings are put on the landscape they appear to offend. Yet cows don't, sheep don't, dogs don't, trees don't, and flowers don't, no matter what their colours or what their shapes, whether it's calm, whether the wind's blowing, whether the trees are blowing about, whether it's autumn, spring, summer or winter; Nature has a way of integrating its own objects into the landscape. Can we do this consciously as human beings? Of course we can. We can give just as much attention to a street lamp, or a litter bin, or a bus station, or a bus shelter, or a house, or the colour of a house, or the colour of a brick. If we do this, then our tenants can have complete freedom to choose whatever coloured curtains they like. It's only if we choose the wrong bricks and paint the doors wrongly that we will get our yellow door clashing with their lavender curtains. Then we should think about our houses in the winter time. It will be dark, the curtains will be drawn, and inside the rooms will be lit up; how will they look? In the summer time they will have no lights on. These details are essentially of the mind of the artist and this is why I need to try to direct the discussion towards the creation of a city in the image of Athens and Florence and Rome.' In no sense was this pretentious. These were cities which were created out of the minds of men who knew what it was they were about. They were consciously created, and by the construction techniques of the time inevitably created out of the products that were available to them. The builders could not carry the stone and the bricks for miles and therefore every area expressed the materials that were natural to that area. This was the kind of message I tried to communicate to my colleagues, and perhaps I was a bad communicator. Maybe I should have had McLuhan looking over my shoulder and doing a spot of prompting. Because, while the Scotswood Road folk responded warmly, my own colleagues were, on the whole, disinterested. So we subsequently were delivered of a new Scotswood Bridge which is a visual monstrosity. Shovelling its double line of cars and lorries into Scotswood Road it eases a traffic bottleneck and creates an eyesore. Well, I'm resigned to being a loser— sometimes.

8

WORKING FOR LEISURE

M Y W A Y of relaxing is to work, and if that sounds paradoxical it is only because I believe that to achieve true leisure one has to take the trouble to strip off one's everyday gear and slip on the pair of creative overalls which hangs behind everyone's door. Unless one makes the effort to effect this metaphorical transition from 'duty' to relaxation, then spare time becomes illusory. An individual has to work at being free.

If this is true for an individual, it is equally so for a community. I tried to make this point in a paper I gave to the Town Planning Institute at its 34th Annual Spring meeting in Newcastle in 1960. When referring to the Blaydon Races centenary which was then two years distant, I said the Newcastle Housing Committee was to celebrate the event by initiating a festival. Its aim was to embrace all aspects of local and regional activities in the fields of art, music, drama, sport, theatre and recreation. Why on earth should a housing committee concern itself with this? Primarily, I suppose, because I was its chairman and it was my only executive position at that time! My belief has always been that a concern for things other than the mundane and workaday can often have a qualitatively heightening effect on the region. The arts can and should play an important part in attracting to the region those people who are interested in them. And if this is true today, it was even more so when Labour came to power in 1958. At that time the theatre was dying, and it very quickly became obvious to me that in Newcastle it was almost 'curtains'. Because I

68

believed in public enterprise, I said to Winston Hand, the city Property Surveyor, 'Let's get among the theatres and try to acquire them. At least, we must keep one theatre going, and then we can formulate a policy for the building of a new theatre in the city.' So we bought the Palace Theatre, a large music hall, amidst a tremendous outcry from the press and a lot of other people because we paid £80,000 for it. I imagine that today, if we bought it, we would pay nearer a quarter of a million. It was a good investment in terms of the acquisition of land, and I do not think that is a bad thing. I think that 'land for the people' is a good slogan at any time. Equally we put feelers out to the Empire Theatre, which was owned by Moss Empires. We pushed through the acquisition of that rather fine music hall at a cost of something like £140,000. Subsequently it has been demolished and the site redeveloped in co-operation with private enterprise. That left us with the Theatre Royal, Newcastle's legitimate theatre, owned by Howard and Wynd-ham, and the Playhouse. The Playhouse, a repertory establish-ment, suffered from the fact that for much of its life it had been concerned almost exclusively with non-demanding popular attractions which people would be prepared to go and see. Until more recently, it really made no influential contribution to drama in the North-East. It was more a reflection of the theatre in decline, than of an exciting and adventuresome organisation.

I took the view that it was important to develop a positive policy for the theatre in Newcastle, and I talked at length to John Neville who was at that time keen to leave London and play a part in the provinces. I talked also to Adrian Cairns who was at that time with our local Tyne-Tees Television, and with as many others as I could. I needed the ideas of people who believed in the theatre. Eventually I began to get clearly in my mind what kind of role drama could play, and the wider role of the arts in general also fell into place in my thinking. If the arts could be based soundly on education, not only in Newcastle, but on Wearside and Teesside, then we could begin to build creative leisure in the Northern Region. Being a politician, of course, I was not completely starry-eyed. I had a fairly clear idea of public intervention both as an opportunity and a danger. I remember saying at the time that we did not want 'Swan Lake' to become a corps-de-ballet of municipal jackbooters. And this was a danger. Instead of creating a liberal arts movement we could easily have councillors dancing around forbidding this and that because they did not like it, or because they sensed that it was too avant-garde. I could see this danger back in 1958 and I see it also in 1970. But ten years ago my concern was to get a regional Arts Association formed.

Admittedly the idea had been kicked around nationally without any success for several years. In the North, Eustace Percy had flown an arts kite from around about 1950. He had seen the possibilities of the Nye Bevan sixpenny rate but had not got very far. Then one day I received a call from Charles Bosanquet, the Vice-Chancellor of the University of Newcastle, asking if I would go along to see him. Tall and bespectacled, he said, 'I wonder what we can do for the arts in Newcastle and the North?' Then he outlined to me his ideas. I said, 'This is absolutely spot-on. If you feel like that, we'll get ahead with the idea.' Then I began to think, 'How do you get ahead with it? It's not a popular theme. The arts don't make as much money as business and they aren't as necessary as sewers.' So once more I set off on my customary ploy, stumping the country to canvass the best ideas from which a formula could be devised. Eventually I was clear on the kind of organisation we wanted in the North. I felt I could see the way it might work, and prognosticate its timing and direction.

So I went to see the Labour Lord Mayor who in 1959 was Kate Scott. She was sympathetic but was very much involved in her own important work for the World Refugee Campaign and could not spare time for my ideas. So I had to lie low for twelve months until Gladys Robson was Lord Mayor. She had a sympathetic spot for the arts, and was receptive to my advocacy. So on the municipal front I spent time persuading

Gladys that the establishment of an arts organisation was an objective that she should pursue during her year of office. On the political front I showed Joe Eagles the paper I had prepared on the subject. I said to him, 'The problem here is money. The best thing to do is to approach the chairman of the Finance Committee and breathe the words into his mouth. If we can get Ted Fletcher's support, then we're in business.' So we spoke to Ted and he readily accepted the idea because he was a man who appreciated the arts. We then put him in the same field as Vice-Chancellor Bosanquet, and allowed their minds to mate. Out of this mating came a mayoral conference of people who were interested in establishing a North Eastern Association for the Arts, and so it was born. And at that stage I stood back. I watched it from the wings and saw it gather momentum.

From our selfish point of view we had the good fortune to see Arthur Blenkinsop lose his seat in parliament, for he was the ideal helmsman to steer the North East Association for the Arts through the rapids of its early course. As far as I was concerned, I saw the Association as the further development of the long-established People's Theatre. I saw it as a natural flow of the convictions of ordinary people that a society that could not sustain and make the arts flourish was a society that would die. And therefore I had clearly in my mind that it was not only essential that we had in Newcastle a college of art and industrial design, but that we should also have colleges of music and drama for serious students and for interested amateurs. And all the time I was trying to spread the message that through these educative and enriching activities we would build a firm foundation on which to erect the region's economy.

But of course, for many people in the North, leisure is synonymous with sport, and as a keen sportsman myself I was anxious to see the region's sporting facilities expanding. This was not easy. We launched our famous argument with Newcastle United in 1958 and it went on until 1962. I do not think now that it will ever be fought to a successful conclusion. What we on the council were saying was that if the future of the North-East lay in Europe, and if the connections between Newcastle and the Scandinavian countries were right, then the same concept was absolutely clear in the world of soccer, which had to be seen in a European context. It makes me smile now, when Europe is looked upon as the prerogative of Newcastle United. But our arguments went beyond that, because we were pointing out that the city's football club lay on the inner periphery of an area of some 20,000 young people who were going to be living within a comparatively short distance of the ground in the education precinct. Therefore, if we could harness the energies of those young people who wanted to take part in sport, to the opportunities which the club could offer to intelligent players who wished to become trainers, coaches and P.E. teachers, then we had a link which could enhance sport, education and leisure. If we could add a good, well-designed multi-sports centre, available for seven days a week, we could set the sports world on fire. We interested Ove Arup in the project. He was an expert and an internationalist. But with the club, we failed. We failed because the management of Newcastle United was like the management of so many other British clubs; it was complacent. It had tremendous support from the rank and file of the population in the North. Football is the ballet of Tyneside, every man understands it, and will go through thick and thin to watch it. His stoic and faithful thesis is that he will stand in the wet for 50 years to watch 'the lads', provided something is dished up. He did not have the desire to press the club forward towards improvements; yet Newcastle is potentially one of Britain's wealthiest clubs. Many poorer clubs in England have superior facilities. But, persistent as ever, I said, 'Right, we'll have a meeting in the City Hall and invite the public'. So we had a meeting and only about 1300 people turned up. It was quite a good meeting, but it did not really get off the ground because the argument was whether we were right to use ratepayers' money in that kind of discussion. And equally, of course, I knew that the press had a vested interest in football. It is one of the best-sellers of newspapers, and I suppose that in the case of the Newcastle *Evening Chronicle* there were still memories of the days when Colin Veitch was prevented from travelling with the team because of speaking out of turn. It struck me that the latter-day soccer correspondents were a little wary of objective assessment of the St. James's Park scheme, lest the club might deny them the kind of facilities that they needed.

So, Newcastle could have possessed one of the finest major European sports centres in a temperate climate. It could have rivalled that of Real Madrid, or even a modest Aztec Stadium. But the argument was never joined. There seemed always to be the feeling in the Board Room that United could get away with providing second-rate facilities. It is a matter of regret to me now that the university and the city are prepared to countenance this. If we had not fought that battle, local people might care to reflect that, facing the magnificent sweep of Leazes Terrace there would today be the alternative erection which United proposed: a corrugated asbestos stand, unpainted, and as true to the traditions of a great football club as would be a patch of clover in the lawns of Kew. We are spared that horror, but we have the floodlighting pylons as a constant reminder that insensitivity is not an offence in the F.A. handbook. A little-publicised gesture made by the city council to Newcastle United was an offer to have the 21-year lease of St. James's Park extended to 60 years. This required the introduction of a clause in a special parliamentary bill, and it was gladly conceded by the city without any sign of reciprocity.

So a chance was lost, but at least the formation of a Sports Association to match our Arts Association, enabled integration and development of this important area of leisure pursuits to go ahead. And later, when Labour gained control at Westminster, I was delighted when Denis Howell, knowing of our good intentions in the North, asked me if I would serve on the National Sports Council. I said that I would for a number of reasons, although by that time I was not fit. I had had two heart attacks and I could not exactly participate in sport. But I had

a background of climbing and walking, and I had canoed and
played soccer, cricket and tennis. Never had I done any of
these things well, but I had enjoyed them. I had had a go!
My motivation in accepting Denis Howell's offer was that I
might be able to play some part in building up a regional
Sports Council philosophy. So I joined the Sports Council and
had many useful discussions. I like to think that I played some
part in formulating ideas, and in giving some encouragement to
people like Walter Winterbottom. I also had the opportunity
of working with people like Roger Bannister and Cliff Morgan.
Denis Howell was a good Minister for Sport, and the country
owes him a lot.

One of the happier perks was a reception we had at
10 Downing Street, where we met a host of sportsmen. As a
follow-up to that I wrote an allegedly humorous article for
Punch with lots of name-dropping and casual references to
Henry Cooper and Georgie Best and their ilk. What genuinely
intrigued me in meeting these sportsmen was their absorption
in leisure rather than work. But to them, of course, work was
leisure. And this common denominator of enjoyable dedication
clearly ran through from sport to art—from sportsmen of all
kinds to artists of all types. Moreover, with my experience of
fostering developments in education and planning and housing,
I could see the bonds which linked all professionals. How
sensible it was for educationalists to talk to planners! How
necessary for ballet dancers to communicate with footballers.
How natural for scientists and architects to explain to each
other the dilemmas and joys of their disciplines. Through the
sixties I took every opportunity to lecture and talk on this theme
of the interdependence of work and leisure. This brought
me into contact with people like Barbara Hepworth and
Henry Moore. I was able to draw on wider and wider
experience.

One of the things I treasure is an article about me in which
I was quoted on my taste in music. I had said it depended on
my mood. Sometimes I liked Constable and Beethoven and at

other times I liked Picasso and Bartok. It boiled down to whether I felt like being consoled or stimulated. A few days later I received an inscribed record from Yehudi Menuhin, which I treasure. It was Bartok's Concerto for Violin and Orchestra. On the sleeve was written : 'To Dan Smith to spur you on your excellent way, and hope we may meet some day to discuss Bartok and Buildings'. Subsequently I did meet him, and in conversation it seemed that my ideas of the relationship between Picasso and Bartok were getting off the ground. They were not just clichés. And in the sixties too, there was evident in the field of the arts, an outgoing regional consciousness. The North Eastern Association for the Arts was making its mark. When Glyndebourne came to Newcastle I smiled to myself, for one of the carrots I had held out in that paper in 1960 had been that Newcastle could become a city where touring opera companies such as Glyndebourne might visit. I thought, 'Right, Glyndebourne has visited, and if people think these things happen accidentally, why should I worry?' Because in the end, sometimes after a long time, things happen, if you understand why they should happen. And you can inspire people who are in a position to make them happen. It was very, very important to my own method of working both in leisure and in politics. I was, after all, a politician, I was interested in power because I knew you could not do anything without it.

You could not take through a fully rounded-out philosophy unless you had the power to round it out, because it was always an investment in those things that really mattered to people, where investment was cut. Unless you had power, you could depend on it, it would be the library book that would go whether it was in the education system or the public library system. It would be the painting that would not be bought. It wouldn't be the road sweeper who did not sweep the streets. That would be the last thing to go. So to provide an enhanced cultural and recreational environment in the North I had to play a Jekyll and Hyde role of assessing as sensitively as I could the needs and aspirations of those I served, and then putting on my political hat and fighting for them. In this way we bulldozed through a competition for sculptors on Scotswood Road on the theme of the emergence of the region from the Industrial Revolution. At the same time we commissioned work, such as the family groups in Shieldfield, and play sculpture. All controversial, of course, but designed to draw people's attention to the role of the artist. And our bludgeoning strategy in the city council began to result in money finding its way into the budget for the Civic Centre. Admittedly the role of the artist never became integrated into the city's strategic thinking as I would have wished, but even its recognition in a somewhat gimmicky form, in the artistic attributes of our new city Civic Centre, was a heartening step forward. All across the board we were stimulating interest in the arts and leisure. We were giving money to the North Eastern Association for the Arts, we were encouraging the Northern Sinfonia Orchestra and wooing Boris Brott, and we were at all times trying to get our Northern Region to realise that while on the one hand the importance of jobs and prosperity is undisputed, there is still a need for enriching leisure. I think that, as time passed, we struck a reasonably happy balance between the conflicting needs of individuals. We fought hard for evicted families, for slum clearance, for the artist, for leisure, for recreation, and for Sunday morning football. Protagonists of these or any other human cause could depend on a sympathetic hearing from our council. We tried to take our leisure seriously!

9

THE REGION

THE PLANE taxied slowly across the tarmac in front of the shoddy, run-down buildings which in 1964 comprised Newcastle's air-passenger terminal at the city's Woolsington Airport. Weaving its way around the perimeter track it provided an occasional port-hole view of the site where the magnificent new terminal was to be built. The engines juddered as, port and starboard, they boosted the aircraft's leisurely progress. Then the end of the runway was reached. A sharp 90° swivel and we were facing south, the smooth expanse of concrete leading our eyes forward to the furthest extremity of the airfield. Held against the brakes while the revs were piled on, we were straining to shake off our sea-level shackles. It was time to be up and away. Then we were moving. Car-like at first, so that a swift disorientation from the suspicion that traffic lights might turn to red at the next corner, was not possible. Then immediate recognition as the tyres bounced, the wings tilted ever so slightly, and the runway recoiled and sulked off. At once we were over the suburbs of Newcastle. Northumberland Street, Elswick Road and Claremont Place were mere slits in a grey Lilliput. The Tyne ditch with its Meccano bridges writhed to the sea. And then, as we brushed the low-lying cumulus, the whole of the North-country offered itself to us. Towns and moors, rivers and forests, coasts and lakes. Counties cut down to size and parochial jealousies ironed out. If ever there was a revelation of togetherness, this was it. We of the

North were not just town or country or city dwellers. We were people of a region.

That Friday, Ada and I were flying to London. From there we were to visit Rome, and return to London on the following Tuesday. Across the plane gangway from me was an old friend—Ted Short. He was off to London too and was in high spirits. After all, a Labour victory had just been declared in the 1964 General Election. He talked of his ideals for the new Parliament, and I mentioned that I was also due to meet George Brown during the following week. Our respective horizons were widening, his to national concerns, mine to regional.

The paper I had given in 1960 on the subject of the regional capital was just a drawing-together of threads, all of which were concerned with regional policy. It was clear that the three political parties were beginning to search for such a policy. The Liberals in particular were beginning to make a strong play for devolution of power. Then came two significant developments, one which could have been anticipated, and the other which was less obvious. The former was the decision by Harold Macmillan to send Lord Hailsham north. Whatever the reasoning behind this decision, many of us suspected at the time that it was connected with the need to win seats in the North. The Conservative government wanted to retain power, and this made sense. It is interesting that a man like Hailsham came north, and with his perceptive mind which could range right across the board, grasped immediately the main problems. During a series of visits he made an impact which was quite fundamental. His call was for a concentration on investment, in jobs and communications, and for the implementation of a growth area policy. Hailsham not only understood road communication; he was quick to see the importance of air communication. He realised the worthwhileness of recreation. It was during his time here that the Regional Sports Council got under way; he also appreciated the arts as a regional catalyst. For the first time I was able to see a liberal-minded Conservative, with a knife-keen mind, operating on problems in a region where such problems had defied solution from the thirties up to 1963 when he was in the North. As Lord Chancellor, he should serve Ted Heath well. My blunt reaction was, 'Yes, this is all very fine, but sign a cheque.' It was almost as crude as that. I remember making a similar point in the Admiralty in Whitehall, when Downing Street was being renovated, in relation to the arts in the North. After the meeting Harold Macmillan cornered me and talked for several minutes on the subject. And this when almost every other contribution had been about employment.

It was the beginning of national recognition that man does not live by job alone; certainly this was a pronounced feature of Hailsham's approach. He appreciated the necessity for changing a backward region such as ours into an advanced region, and sowing within the policy field the seeds of our own growth, rather than having to be continually dependent on outside aid. I think therefore that his contribution is to be measured not in terms of millions of pounds invested in motorways, but rather as a crucial step forward in regional thinking on the broadest possible front. These qualities together with his legal background should make him a great Lord Chancellor. During that time also, in the grass-roots Labour Party, there had been developing a sense of dissatisfaction with the way in which regional policy was lagging. Particularly was this true in Glasgow, Liverpool and here on Tyneside, all development areas, and all outward-looking areas.

At Liverpool there was Alderman Bill Sefton. He was an ordinary working lad who was the leader of Liverpool Council. In Glasgow there was an equally outstanding person, Peter Meldrum, who was also of working-class origin, and possessed of a good brain. We knew each other, and decided that we had much in common. So we said, 'Well, what can we do? No-one can stop us from meeting over the frontiers.' So we had a conference, convened by the Lord Mayor of Newcastle, to allow the regions to exchange views. At the same time I submitted to

George Brown a paper advancing the claims of a policy for the regions. This was set against the background of the reluctance of several Conservative ministers to consider the radical re-organisation of local government. The issue was gradually moving into the political arena, and people's prejudices were showing.

In examining regionalism I always need to try to look at the topic in the context of the white-hot technological revolution. There was a feeling in the early sixties different from the widely-based mass movement of people's minds in 1945, opposed to the philosophic doldrums of the pre-war years. In the sixties we had an elite movement. It was a reflection of the greater number of working-class people who by then were beginning to shine in the fields of science and technology. Their concern was about the quality of life and environment, about clean rivers and good housing. They reflected the consciousness of our age of increasing leisure, and they were articulate exponents of devolution and regionalism. As the concept of a Department of Economic Affairs was developing, so was political thinking about the reform of local government. Because we in the North were in the vanguard, the leaders of the Labour Party came north to talk to us in Newcastle and to look at the pioneering efforts we were making. They were good listeners. The DEA concept emerged first, and from this there sprang Regional Economic Planning Councils. These councils seemed to me at the time to be temporary organisations only. I could see no permanent response to regional aspirations other than a full reform of local government. But this interim decision on the regions was the right one. I think that the non-elected provincial council at that time was, and today still remains, a valid, transitional organisation pointing towards the devolution of power. It will gather momentum after the reform of local government, get into top gear when Britain takes a decision on whether she is going into Europe, and coast home a real winner when Crowther's Constitutional Commission produces its findings. It all takes time. The thinking has gone on for almost

ten years in the Labour Party. I recently chaired a Labour
Party committee which contained quite a number of former
cabinet ministers and which issued a report on the next stage
of regionalism. This does not mean that progress will necessarily
be swift, but there will be seen to be a clear progression of
thinking and ideas.

A conference which I attended in Prague in 1969 made clear
to me that the problems we are grappling with here are common
to Eastern and Western European countries. To some extent
they echo across the world. In Prague I contributed a minor
paper; it was factual rather than philosophical, but from discussion which ensued, I could sense that the world is moving
into a period of regionalism. One recalls the old BBC slogan
that region shall speak peace unto region. It has a darn sight
more chance of being successful than the more ambitious and
ill-conceived notion that nation shall speak peace unto nation.
These were the reflections that were passing through my mind
as I flew to London on that Friday of high hopes. The Department of Economic Affairs was a reality with George Brown
at its head. And he wanted me to take a job.

Ada and I met George and his wife on the evening of the
following Tuesday. We spent some time in discussion and he
applied some pressure on me to take a job in London with the
DEA. It was a dilemma for me because I was naturally tempted.
I was a supporter of the government and I wanted the DEA
to succeed in its regional policies. But I felt that to move to
London would not be consistent with my conviction that some
people have to stay in the region. They still have opportunities
to communicate with the centre. I felt that insofar as I was
identified as a regional character by this time, it was important
that I stayed in my neck of the woods. But the day that the
Labour government was elected I was thrown into the melting
pot of reorganisation of departments concerned with local
government and regional policy, and George wanted me to
contribute decisively. I remember saying to him that in my
experience you could not treat civil servants in the way that he

was asking me to treat them. What standing had I got? He said, 'Well, I'll ring them up', and he picked up the phone and rang the department. It was late, but he must have thought they worked all night. Anyhow, there was no-one there, so he told me to ring up McIntosh in the morning and inform him that the minister wanted me to discuss the kind of ideas I had for regional policy. My response was that I would do it, but that my ideas would not be acceptable to civil servants because they were not convinced that regions were viable units. Even if they did become convinced they would not appreciate some Geordie off the streets telling all about it. But that was a period of advisers and consultants. Men like Balogh and Kaldor were drafted into government, and did a good job. So, in some trepidation, I rang up McIntosh the next morning. He had been with Hailsham as one of the key members of his team. I went in and said, 'I was talking to George Brown last night and he suggested various matters.' I could see at once that the reaction was not very enthusiastic. Especially were there no cries of delight at the thought of T. Dan Smith playing some part in a reorganisation. It was what I anticipated, because during the Hailsham days I was not aware of McIntosh's interest in the development of regions and DEA's, although it became clear to me later on that he had been quite active in these fields with George Brown.

The man I confided in most of all was James, the chief planner in the Ministry of Housing and the man who I think more than anybody, was responsible for the view of the civil service on local government. He was chief planner and knew town halls inside out. He had worked with Lady Evelyn Sharp for a good number of years ; he more than anybody else was responsible for the city regional concept of local government which later on, when the Maud Commission was established, expressed his views on city regions. They were, as it turned out, minority views, but nevertheless sound.

I was able to talk to him, because although he was of the Establishment, he was not a normal civil servant. He had been born at Byers Green. His father and my father lived in the same street. We came from the same background and I remember well the night he got his government appointment. We went out and wined and dined magnificently. Neither of us could be said to be gourmets or drinkers, but you can imagine that we had a very happy evening. And why was this? Because he was the first man to be appointed planner from an arts background rather than from an economic planning background. He had this tremendous understanding of the problems of regions such as ours, although he would probably be best known because of his South-East Study which was produced under the Conservative government. So he was a tremendous help to me in understanding the civil servant's mind. He recognised in our Newcastle experiments something meaningful.

Under Richard Crossman, when he was Minister of Housing, the notion of reforming local government became a really revolutionary look at the structure of Britain. Unfortunately, of course, what we did not know as we flew south on our plane from Newcastle was that the Labour majority was as low as four. Many dreams had to remain dreams. This was unfortunate, because Britain had not much time in my view; it had already wasted ten years that could have been spent on the thinking-through and reorganisation of local government. After all, we in Newcastle had had the experience of the Boundary Commission Report on Tyneside. I had managed to convince my colleagues that what Newcastle should be was a regional capital. To be a regional capital it had to have a local government structure. This tore to shreds the leadership of the Labour council in Newcastle which had come out for four county boroughs for Tyneside. There were some ding-dong arguments, but in any case political events dictated that nothing could happen until either the Labour government was confirmed in power by another election, or alternatively thrown out of power. So I applied all the energy and influence that I had in an attempt to get Tyneside Unification approved. After all, we had Teesside unification, and I felt that if we could get both Tyne and Tees in the forefront nationally, we could lead the country. We could really forge full speed ahead in advance of local government reform, and show what the devolution of power could yield.

Teesside got away with it; Tyneside rested in the hands of Richard Crossman. I went to Crossman's house with Ted Short and spent some time discussing the issues with him. Crossman has a tremendous intellectual capacity. After a pleasant family meal with him, I felt that he was 'sold' on my ideas, and I returned to Newcastle thinking, 'Well, that's a good day's work done for Tyneside.' The tragedy of it was, of course, that Crossman did not stay in his ministry long enough. He was replaced by Tony Greenwood. Crossman had decided that as soon as Labour was consolidated in political power the Royal Commission on Local Government Reform would be set up and Tyneside would go ahead of the field with Teesside. Then he moved ministries. Shortly after, the Royal Commission was established. I was one of its members. Ironically, once I was wearing my Commission hat, I could not fight for Tyneside unification. My loyalties were divided and torn. A great opportunity slipped away. I remember Crossman saying quite angrily that this was a great tragedy for Tyneside.

What happened then? We had Regional Economic Councils established and we had George Brown as the boss. It is generally known that George is not the most discreet of people. He used to come north when the Durham Miners' Gala was on; it was on his beat. I often used to run him down to the Durham Gala when he flew up from London on the Friday. I always brought him back from the Gala to the airport. By the time George had spent a full day in Durham, he was invariably in a jovial mood, and on one such occasion he made it quite clear that he wanted me to be chairman of the Economic Planning Council in the North, and equally he felt that it would be better if I gave up my work on the Newcastle City Council in order to devote it to the Economic Planning Council field. He wanted me to get the concept of the role of the Regional Economic Planning

Council rooted within the Northern Region, in association with local government.

10

THE PLANNING COUNCIL

THAT T. DAN SMITH was to be the head of the new Economic Planning Council seemed to be common knowledge long before the official announcement was made. This was due to George Brown's habit of thinking aloud. His 'leaks' tended to be titanic. And as soon as the word got around, the usual anti-Smith lobby slotted into gear. Those who came out most strongly against me were not Tories but members of my own regional Labour Party. They were so incensed at the thought that I might get the job that they sent a deputation to London to see if they could not spike my guns. To George Brown's credit, he not only stuck to his point of view, but gave them a few home truths. When they came back, I was somewhat mollified to see them overruled by their executive when they met in full session. Thereafter I enjoyed the support of the regional Labour Party, but there remained a natural niggle. What does one do to get the kind of support one needs in order to carry through a job? I never understood why people felt badly disposed to me. Perhaps they could not reconcile my rumoured 'millionaire' status with my socialist beliefs. There was no need for them to do so. Not only am I not a millionaire; I am a man of modest means. But a number of them had conceived an image of me as somebody who was in the power game for what he could get out of it. This hurt me. Others doubtless felt that I could not do the job. This I could accept. It was up to me to prove them wrong—I am pretty certain that if the government had put forward a big name to lead the NEPC my critics would have jumped at it. Anyone rather than Dan Smith!

So I went into the job with some misgivings. Around my heels my detractors were yapping. Over my shoulder was the prospect of a unified Tyneside. Enough seats had been put in the new Civic Centre to act as a regional parliament. No-one asked us why 124 seats had been installed, but my thinking had been that this was just about right for a regional parliament. Now I had to forget about that. In the event Tyneside was not unified, my critics called off the hunt, and I could get on with my new job.

Of course I knew that I was, in a sense, committing political suicide. Since 1958 I had been chairman of most of the major committees on the city council, and for the past five years I had been its leader. My role had become that of a catalyst—a shaper of policy. With a policy advisory committee fulfilling cabinet-like functions, and a city manager appointed, Newcastle could lead the country with a new style of local government. And I could be at the centre of things, helping to organise people's brains, and clearing away bureaucratic deadwood. Did it make sense to leave all this for a rather ill-defined regional fledgling, which was to have no executive powers?

On the whole I thought that it did. The decision taken by the government in the early months of 1965 to establish Economic Planning Councils was public recognition of the importance of regions, and of the necessity to combine economic and physical planning. The First Secretary of State intended that they should play an active role and take the initiative in raising issues at government level. It seemed like a new and exciting challenge, and an opportunity to speak for the North to a larger, national audience. This business of interpreting my neck of the woods to other Englishmen has always been a problem. In 1967 I was writing, tongue in cheek, in *Punch*: 'The southerner is, almost without exception, ignorant of the North. If a population drift northwards is to be encouraged, we must inform southerners of the people with whom they are

going to fraternise. We initiated a recent survey to give us a
basis on which to work, and this is what we discovered : One
per cent knew definitely that Newcastle upon Tyne was a
village surrounded by 83 pit heaps. The other 99 per cent
thought it was a suburb of Harlow New Town. Seventy-nine
per cent believed that the northerner kept coals in his bath ;
11 per cent knew this to be nonsense, and with modern
education they were certain that he kept smokeless fuel in his
bath. Six per cent were of the opinion that there were no baths
north of Potter's Bar. The vast distances which separate Marble
Arch from Newcastle's Grey's Monument must be bridged by
spreading, increasing knowledge. We must strive to let our
people know as much about Northern England as they already
do about Korea, China, Vietnam and Egypt—we may even
have to contemplate opening an emigration office in Piccadilly
to inform the emigrants of the new life and new opportunities
of the North.'

And if you think that is satire, try asking a cockney if Newcastle
United play in the first or second division of the Scottish League !

But now I saw an opportunity of speaking out more
prominently and effectively for my region. So I swapped hats,
moved office a quarter of a mile, and sat down in front of a
clear desk-top for the first time in years.

The DEA was setting up similar regional organisations in
various parts of England as well as in Wales and Scotland.
I was lucky in being allocated a senior civil servant, Jim
Robertson, who was the British civil servant at his best. He was
possessed of a tremendous personality, and was also kind and
intellectually gifted. He could work with people. He knew how
to weld a team of new boys into a functioning organization.
Here he was, moulding an Economic Planning Board in a part
of Britain that he did not know too well, and in a department
of the DEA that was raw, unstructured and suspect. He accepted
the challenge coolly, and his self-composure helped to boost my
confidence.

For I was nervous. This was new, uncharted territory. My

initial forays would have to be tentative and circumspect. I could not afford to put my foot in it. I was on the spot.

One of my first jobs was to identify those areas of activity where the Northern Economic Planning Council infringed on existing organizations or elected bodies. There was the Federation of British Industries, now the CBI, and there was the Regional TUC Advisory Committee which had always been consulted by the government. My feeling was that although their discussions were worthy, they did not really scratch the surface of the North's economic problems. But they were, nevertheless, a local power structure and they were led by Sir Mark Hodgson, a father-figure in the area, who rightly merited respect and tactful handling. He had concerned himself with items like hotel accommodation and air services, amongst other important issues, and saw no reason for forfeiting these interests.

Then there were local authorities, planning authorities and universities. Their duties and powers and constitutional proprieties had to be respected. And the wisdom of their servants had to be drawn upon when considering membership of the Planning Council. The Minister consulted me about the 25 appointments which were to be made, and liaison was close. A consensus of views was eventually reached. I had reservations about one appointment only and was subsequently overruled. And rightly as it turned out. Not that any selection was easy. There were so many talented and eminently well-qualified people in the North. My concern was to assess the collective character of my Council. How would its members work as a group? Would their specialisms inhibit integration? Their gifts result in friction? Their individualism kill communication? And this raised in my mind the whole question of how one can, through democratic processes, choose the best team to meet the challenge of the times.

The loss of a seat in a by-election can mean the forfeiture of a key person in a national or local administration. The fickleness of voters on a marginal issue can result in the non-return of a brilliant candidate. In the seventies I believe that politicians and people alike will have to face the fact that, in an age of increasing complexity, slogans, barnstorming and party loyalty are not enough. There must be a nucleus of leaders in different fields of human activity who are, in a sense, an elite. And there must be a continuum of policy, without about turns every five years or so. Otherwise, how can ordinary people participate as they should? How can they have time to weigh policies in the balance and make reasoned responses? Participation has nothing to do with shot-gun policies.

In choosing my Planning Council I was faced by such imponderables. I am still perplexed by them. What I am clear about is that one cannot have an unenlightened democracy. Instead, people would opt out of democracy, and larger services would go to appointed rather than elected boards. The Health Service would go, National Parks, water resources and ports would disappear to such boards; major highways, the arts and progressive education would melt away. And one would be left with a whole series of super-organisations with specialized responsibilities, efficiently run, but remote from people. This is repugnant to me. My public work has always been based on a democratic formulation of policy, the communication of this policy to people, the discussion of it by people, and its eventual implementation on behalf of people. I was intent on seeing this philosophy eventually carried through to regional level.

So one can imagine the trepidation that I felt about the first meeting of the new Planning Council. I knew I was going to be the captain of a team of captains. In fact, every individual on the Council was either chairman or chief executive or a leader of an important organisation. One could dare to say that we ranged from top executives to a professor of a university. That did not seem bad for the rank and file. But I looked over my shoulder at my own background of rote learning at the Richardson Dees School in Wallsend, and I felt some insecurity. Moreover, I had heard rumours that a noble lord in Cumberland had advised his colleagues that it was a fate worse than death to

At Richardson Dees School, Wallsend
(*Sun*)

On Tyne Bridge, 1964

Ted Short, Gladys Robson, George Kenyon, Roy Thomson
(*Northern Echo*)

With Dame Evelyn Sharp and a model of Scotswood Road
re-housing, 1961

(*Newcastle Chronicle and Journal*)

At 62 Holly Avenue, Wallsend, March 1968

With Maurice Foley and Roy Jenkins, July, 1966
(*Northern Echo*)

With Frank Cousins and Dan McGarvey
(*Newcastle Chronicle and Journal*)

serve under my chairmanship. So I braced myself for the ordeal,
encouraged at least by the reflection that the event would be
unique. I was certainly determined to establish the fact that
I could run a meeting firmly and competently.

I remember one member of the Council, a well-known figure
locally, who was quite determined at that first meeting that he
should have been chairman and who was going to make it
difficult for me if he could. I steeled myself, turned to him and
said, 'Look, if we're all going to be chairman at this meeting
we're not going to get very far. While many of you may have
views as to whether I should have been the chairman, I am
appointed, and if we've got a job to do we can only do it if we
work efficiently. That is how I intend to work.' Thereafter,
and without any qualifications at all, these meetings were the
most efficient that I have ever had the privilege to chair. Quickly
I broke the council down into working parties and briefed them
to set about preparing a regional plan for the North, within the
national plan. As it turned out, *The Challenge of the Changing
North* was a document on which I had a lot of personal influence. Its phraseology, its structure, were the work of those
skilled writers—the civil servants; its contents, ranging from
technology to the arts, was influenced not a little by my own
thinking, and even the design on the front cover had my interest.
That design resulted from many hours of discussion with our
own C.O.I. chief, and equally as much consultation with
advisers at the Central Office of Information in London. I was
determined that the document would be the first of a series of
documents. I was conscious that it was a comprehensive
regional plan and it became increasingly obvious to me that we
would never produce a regional plan with our kind of
machinery. But *The Challenge of the Changing North* breathed
confidence and life, it was an immediate job for my Planning
Council colleagues to get their teeth into, and it was a useful
medium of communication. It was circulated to every organisation with requests for comments, and I spent night after night
and day after day going round the region to organisations

D

talking about it, and talking about the future. I painted the
picture as I saw it of 15 years of hard slog before we in the North
could really hope to achieve the quality of economic and social
environment which would make it possible for us to boast that
regions are what men make them. This was beyond our reach
in '65 and it still is in the seventies. In 1965 the material was
not there from which to create the region. In the case of a city
like Newcastle, one could create it, because the latent pro-
perties, given that scale, were present. But the region demanded
something more. In order to gather ideas for the 15 year slog,
I hit on what I considered to be a bright idea.

In the fifties Roy Thomson had just bought Newcastle's
Kemsley newspapers. The local press is important in our
region, so I determined to meet him and talk to him about
opportunities and problems in the North. I decided to create
the situation where Roy Thomson would be invited to open
the city's Shieldfield flats, unveil a piece of sculpture and
present the prizes for a painting competition which   the
Evening Chronicle had organized for the youngsters. To my
delight, he agreed to come. Now, I thought, having got this far,
I want to shut 20 people in a room with him, without warning
them at all, and when they are in, I want to ask them a
question. The question would be : 'If you had one of the world's
press barons and you were given three minutes in which to ask
his help for the Northern Region, what would you say?' I
primed Bob Clough to have the proceedings printed, and the
idea appealed to him and Roy Thomson. So I had these un-
suspecting guests come along to a meal paid for by Roy
Thomson. Genial and shrewd he welcomed them, and we sat
down. I was at the head of the table. I said, 'Well, gentlemen,
if you think you've been invited here to enjoy your meal, you're
wrong. What you've been invited here for is to tell me in three
minutes what you would say to a press baron in the interests of
the North.' After a somewhat startled silence, the occasion
developed splendidly. Thereafter, I must say if I ever needed
any general discussion on things that troubled me, or advice

on all sorts of matters, Roy Thomson made himself available. On at least one occasion he invited me to speak to his regional editors in Grays Inn Road.

Following our talk-in meal, I felt that the Thomson Press in the Northern Region had a significant part to play in our evolution. As a complement to this, I think that Roy Thomson was impressed by the way in which we were able to translate ideas into reality. As a man of action himself, he sensed that we could get things done.

Meanwhile, I was exploring ways of planting the seeds of regional consciousness in the rich variety of our northern way of life. I talked to Sandy Dunbar, director of the North Eastern Association for the Arts, about changing the organisation's name to the Northern Association for the Arts. I asked him to think carefully about local government reform and the impact which it could have on the arts. If local government was reactionary, it could destroy the arts. If it became systematized into large units, it might not respond to requests for patronage. I also pressed on with a Northern Sports Council, and was determined to have Lord Lonsdale as Chairman. As is usually the case, determination paid off.

I wanted to see the establishment of a Northern Air Council, but here one saw evidence of the internal claims, and perhaps jealousies, of the emerging region. Newcastle vied with Middlesbrough in its airport claims, and there was little support for Carlisle. Eventually, however, I managed to get together representatives of the local authorities surrounding Carlisle. From this meeting there came sufficient support to engender a limited amount of air traffic at Carlisle Airport. There were not many facilities, and the flying hours were not astronomical, but interest had been stirred. My idea was that eventually a Northern Air Council would look for its capital in Manchester or thereabouts, and this again would be a step towards the devolution of power. I still believe this to be right. Before the Edwards Committee was set up, I, together with the Chairman of the Yorkshire and North-West Planning Councils, met

representatives of BEA and BOAC and independent airlines
in Manchester. We talked about the third alternative to London
Airport and the need within our major road network for an
international airport. I began to sense then the importance of
Regional Planning Councils. Region could speak to region in
a national context. If only, like the planes we talked of, one
could really take off, what things might we not achieve!

Meanwhile there was also tourism to be fully developed in the
North Country. With such a superb environmental background,
and with a backcloth of history vivid in its stirring incidents,
we had much to offer visitors from the United Kingdom and
overseas. I was particularly keen to secure an evocation of the
region's historical links with Rome, northern Europe and
Scotland. Here was an opportunity to launch a creative exercise
which, while rooted in the past, had its economic parallel in
our own times. Were we not intent on drawing closer to Europe,
and linking our region commercially and industrially with other
parts of our own country?

I was also conscious of the political awareness of the Scandinavian countries, which found its echo in their tourist
industry. For instance the Swedes stopped allowing their
nationals to visit Greece and Crete when the Greek Junta
assumed power. Likewise, holders of Greek passports did not
find it easy to gain entry to Sweden. It seemed that tourism
was not just a pair of sunglasses and a package tour, but an
integral part of a country's attitudes and way of life. I wanted
the North of England to recognise this, and to develop the all-
round possibilities which it offered. I gave a talk on 'Leisure
in Europe in the year 2000', in which I included ideas designed
to provoke such discussion. I ranged over the development of the
Industrial Revolution in the temperate countries, where
mineral resources had been exploited earliest, and where wealth
had grown fastest. With personal well-being had come the
demand from people in these countries for holidays abroad.
And where did they make for? Mainly for the warm lands
where their sun-deprivation could be compensated. They

wanted something different. But, come the year 2000, it seemed likely that the warm, sub-tropical lands would have achieved their own industrial revolution. Southern Italy, Greece, the North African states and Israel would then have their own ebullient economies, and their people would be eager for holidays abroad. Where would they go? Not in search of the sun, I hazarded. They would want something different. Perhaps, I suggested, our own Roman Wall country, with its mysterious mists and invigorating breezes, would be their goal. Or our castle-strewn Northumbrian coastline, with magnificent beaches uncluttered by deck-chairs, awnings and Mediterranean vulgarity. We had to be ready for this.

In no sense do I claim that my thinking about tourism was either original or significant, nor that others were unaware of the opportunities, but it did seem to me that I would like, on behalf of my region, to share our thoughts with others at national level. So I went to Ted Short, then Chief Whip, and said that I wanted to talk to all the ministers who were involved in tourism and those departments of education which were linked to tourism. I met several of them, including Denis Howell, Jennie Lee and Roy Mason; I talked to them about my concept, but I cannot say that ministers respond collectively as enthusiastically as they do separately. There is a peculiar feeling about ministers collectively. Each of them understands and ploughs his own departmental furrow, and to try to get them to integrate their thinking on regional problems is not easy. What I was trying to say was that just as no one should want to despoil the coasts of the Mediterranean as they are being despoiled because we are going to hand these on to generation after generation of people, so we should be careful in this country to harvest our natural heritage of beauty, and reclaim those despoiled landscapes, many of which lay in my own region. We in Britain should take the lead in an enthusiastic, exciting protection of Europe's beauty, conservation; yes, and creation, even more so. Let every year be conservation year.

Subsequently I was disappointed when I was not included

on the Tourist Board because I felt I had done a lot of work and thinking on the subject. I had talked to Geddes and others about our opportunities, and tried to translate ideas into practical possibilities. There was our own River Tyne, for instance, a proud river, but not one renowned for its pleasant lower reaches. I was sure that, along those ugly banks, we could have international groups of students working. There would be a Swedish section, a Norwegian section, a Dutch section and so on. I felt we could start this enterprise, and at the same time say to our own local youngsters, 'Right, off you go to the Rhine and tidy up there.' So we would develop genuine participation, creativity, and activity amongst young folk.

Now of course, any thinking on tourism in the North of England is bound to involve discussion of the Lake District. My family and I love the Lakes. We used to have a cottage there, and on difficult, end-of-one's-tether days, our thoughts stray to limpid water, gaunt fells and tranquillity. Now Cumberland and Westmorland were part of the Northern Economic Planning Council's area and I wanted to help in the thinking with its people, and do what I could to promote their well-being, so I used to make many journeys by car westwards from Newcastle, up over the Pennines and so into the beautiful counties. And what did I find? Well, I found what one would expect to find—Gentlemen; and a lot of them just did not like the way I worked. They didn't like an outsider coming in to stir up the area. They did not want Solway City, they did not see the potential of the investment in the A6 or in the water resources of the Solway Firth, or the electrification of the Euston-Glasgow line. Equally, they did not like to hear me talking about the historical importance of the city of Carlisle, or of the Roman Wall, and how these formed a basis for the creation of at least one arts centre in Penrith and one at Kendal. They were deaf to suggestions about an extension of the National Park, and the possibility of drawing people out of the National Park to theatres and concert halls. The idea that particularly infuriated them was that of a festival centre. This was an attempt by me to relieve pressure on the natural amenities of the Lakes. It would absorb the interest of many visitors and prove a cultural focal point. Maybe I presented the idea in an ingenuous way. My message was that if one went to the London Palladium presumably it was not to see ballet, but variety. Conversely, if one attended Covent Garden it was not to hear Tom Jones, but to involve oneself in opera. There was, I suggested, a parallel between this fitness of theatrical experience, and the development of National Parks. If we had to provide for leisure, then we had to learn from the experiences of the last hundred years in terms of entertainment, and ensure that the audiences in our natural Covent Garden—which was the way I saw the Lake District—come to expect ballet and not variety. With this in mind we had to plan the provision of artistic facilities. And in doing so we had to match them to the towering majesty of Scafell, the placid calm of Grasmere, and the natural rightness of a grey slate scree. I was not simply wanting to create a festival centre, but to combine the work of the archaeologist, the historian, the poet, the dramatist, the musician and the naturalist. I hoped that by this artistic and educational policy there could be created a place of interest for tourists, students, children and the Lakelanders themselves.

This seemed to me to be quite a reasonable proposition, but it did not meet with universal acclaim. Reactionary people hinted that it was turning the Lake District into a new Blackpool. I knew that it was their negative thinking which would produce a Blackpool. Eventually Keswick will be destroyed by the sheer pressures of human demand to eat, to drink, to go to the toilet, to park cars and to obtain petrol. Of course, there were many people who thought and felt as deeply as I did. Peter Scott of Kendal, who had established the Abbott Hall Gallery, was a stimulating ally. So was Kenneth Steen, the Planning Officer for Cumberland, but we were outnumbered. Not only were we outnumbered by the gentlemen of Cumberland, but also by ordinary chaps from my own sort of background, with whom I found difficulty in communicating on a number of projects. This was strange, for I had known a number of them from earlier days when I was an ILP organiser in the North. They could not understand that I was advocating Solway City as a means of preserving their wonderful natural environment. And there grew up this odd alignment of the country gentlemen and many of the miners and steel-workers of West Cumberland, and especially of Millom. But through all this I stuck to my guns. One great stimulus was my determination not to make concessions to the present. As I saw it, the population explosion means that today will always be outvoted numerically by tomorrow. If my colleagues and I were to create a world for tomorrow, then we had, in a sense, to carry votes for those citizens still in their prams. Yet at the same time, as we were dedicated to participation and persuasion, we had to avoid imposing our personal views. If only one could participate with babies in prams!

Cumberland, of course, had real problems. And I could not see the answer to them in terms that made sense socially, and at the same time economically. In fact Cumberland, and to a certain extent North-West Durham, brought me face to face with what I would call a problem of scale, rather than density. It was, in some ways, like some of the heart-aches I had experienced over Scotswood Road. I had to burn the midnight oil on Scotswood Road because I knew the folk there. Some people referred to them as illiterate dead-beats, but I knew that they included a host of characters and leaders of people. All right, they might not have qualified at the Manchester Business School but they had an understanding of the problems of people and living which psychologists might ponder upon.

I remember the part I took in the first BBC colour film that was made. It included an item on the subject of the Scotswood people and the traumatic experiences felt by them in moving away from their old homes to new estates. With Harold Williamson I went along to talk to an old lady who lived in Railway Street. I was chosen to help Harold in the interviewing because I could talk as she could talk, in her kind of language. She had never been out of Scotswood Road in her life. So I knew that she was talking to me as a person from another world. The prospect of her going to the Newbiggin Hall housing estate was almost like saying to a man who hadn't been trained as an astronaut, 'You're going in the capsule in the morning. Take sandwiches for a ten day trip.' It must have been just about as terrifying. And the problems of West Cumberland were precisely of that kind. How many people were there in Millom like that Scotswood woman? How many were there like her in Workington and Whitehaven? And what was the proposition which faced them? It was in order for Lord Robens and the Coal Board to induce them to move down to Nottingham. That was fair game. But if I suggested that they should go to Carlisle instead, this was not on. So I was trying to say to the West Cumberland folk, 'Look, your children are going to demand of you those things in Cumberland which, unless they are provided, will force them to leave. Even if they are provided they may still leave, but other young people will come in. Therefore, I think we've got to talk about the new Cumberland and the new Cumberland has got to have higher educational facilities, arts, humanities, recreation and real job opportunities.'

I do not think it would be an injustice to anyone to say that I did not get a single torch-carrier except Joe Eagles, who had helped me when he was secretary of the Newcastle Labour Party; he was then in Whitehaven. Once again, I could see in Joe, although almost 20 years older, and therefore not possessed of quite the former fire in his belly, the possibilities of an ally in producing a policy for Cumberland. And we got down to do this, politically, behind the scenes. The crunch-point came at a meeting I held in Workington when I made the statement that I thought there was no future for mining in Cumberland. There was a packed audience which partially accepted my prediction, but the press reacted very sharply against it, and I think misinterpreted my arguments. With local miners' leaders I discussed my prophecy and often I found my

words tinged with the Scotswood Road perspective. Why should
things not be left as they are? Why should industry go to Carlisle
and Penrith? Industry was attracted to Carlisle, and in fact
there were not enough people to work in the factories. So was
the sensible solution not to develop growth areas at Carlisle
and at Solway? Then we could press for colleges of higher
education at Carlisle, recognition for the city's College of Art,
and eventually the creation of an educational complex. I think
Carlisle has great potential for the West Cumbrians, and Britain,
and as a city. But only Joe Eagles really appreciated my arguments, and even he had reservations. Nevertheless, I persisted.
I belted my way through the routines of many ministers who
passed to and fro through Cumberland, including the Prime
Minister. But I could not evoke real support for the growth
area concept. It became increasingly obvious to me that, as
chairman of the Economic Planning Council, I suffered because
of a lack of executive power. I was trying with all the physical
and mental strength that I possessed to postulate what I believed
to be a perfectly honest, straightforward policy. And I was being
compelled to compromise. I could never bring myself to say
to the young folk in Millom that the things they were asking
for were just around the corner. I could not paint a picture
of an easy world where something somehow could be done for
nothing. I found, as month after month went by, and every
meeting I conducted was fraught with argument, discussion
and debate, that I was becoming more and more unpopular.
Then along would come a government minister who would say,
'We'll build an advance factory at Millom.' And this troubled
me. It troubled me because I did not believe it was a policy
for the future, and I did not want to have to advocate that sort
of policy. What I felt it was reasonable to say to the people of
Millom was, 'You won't lose by social change.' Because I was,
as always, determined that the individual would not suffer for
the social good. If necessary, the government should have
spent £10 million in relocating the unemployed people in a
good, thriving environment rather than using the money to

bring industry to them. They and their children would have gained immeasurably in that way.

So I defended my own views and the policies that had been formulated by my Planning Council officials. And this meant a collision course, strangely enough, with another government department—the Board of Trade, which had introduced as a policy the Special Development Areas that meant wherever unemployment was highest, industry should go in, there should be a job created even if the necessary conditions for a full life would never exist. My own concern was with the quality of life, breadth of opportunity, and the concept that concentration on work alone was only a modern equivalent of slavery. It was a case, again, of a failure of communication.

The communication gap was exemplified by an episode which occurred in Cumberland when I was concerned particularly with the problem of the run-down of the local mines. I secured a statement of policy from the North-Western region of the Coal Board, and I accepted it because it made sense. It was a run-down policy, but it was phased in a reasonably humane form, and it seemed reasonable to suppose that the build up of alternative jobs would not fall far short of the run down of the pits. I attended a conference that was convened by Cumberland County Council, I think with a certain political undertone which expressed concern and condemned the government's policy for closing the mines. And, having been convinced by the NCB, I refused to share in the condemnation. I believed the policy to be realistic. When I was asked either by pitman or minister, my answer invariably was, 'Let us get rid of the mining industry. Too many miners' leaders too easily agreed to rapid pit closures—but this was not so in Cumberland. It is an industry of the past.' But this was only a justifiable view when considered in relation to assurances I had received that individuals would not suffer. Almost immediately after I had been to Cumberland and disclosed the policy of mine closures, the Coal Board performed a *volte-face* and I woke up one morning to find a letter announcing that the colliery at Har-

rington, in Cumberland, which had been scheduled to remain
open, was to be closed. It followed from my conviction of the
validity of the principle of participation and consultation, that
this was an unacceptable decision. I had been conscious for
some time that the Ministry of Fuel and Power's machinery
for consultation with the Planning Councils on NCB matters
in North-East England was bad—although safe in the hands
of Bill Reid, Chairman of the NCB, and also a member of the
Planning Council, matters were very different in the North-
West. So my hackles rose, I dug in my heels and said, in effect,
'Right, I have been used as an instrument to deceive Maurice
Rowe, the miners' leader. I have been used as an instrument to
deceive the representatives of those authorities which have been
consulting with me. And I have deceived the miners themselves.'
I went post haste to London to state my grievance, and found
the attitude one that I could not accept. So I said, 'There's
no-one going to give me an assurance concerning people's
livelihoods then alter it without consultation. If an under-
taking is revoked, I demand the right to go back and explain to
the people the reason. If there is no new reason, then I want
to know why the policy has been changed.' I queried furthermore, who decided to close Harrington Colliery 20 days before
Christmas Day? Even if Harrington had to close, there was
no humanity in such a timing. I was indignant. My intro-
spection did a feedback: 'So I'm a kindly man, but I'm tough
too'. On the day in question, a Friday, I was at the Royal
Commission on Local Government Reform in London, and I
tried to get in touch with Peter Shore, and was unsuccessful.
I am not saying this was his fault any more than it was mine,
because ministers are busy people and Fridays are awkward
days when M.P.'s often go out into their constituencies. But I
spoke to Shore's personal assistant who, again, was a decent
chap, but somewhat arrogant that day. I said, 'Now look, I've
spoken to Harold Evans, editor of the *Sunday Times*, and before
I leave London today, I'm going to write an article, and in this
article I'm going to resign as chairman of the NEPC unless I

have some clear indication of the procedures to be followed in the nationalised industries which affect the communities in which I am involved. In doing so, I can do more in resignation than I have been able to do in the actual job.' The civil servant's response was something to the effect that circumstances which precipitate articles in Sunday newspapers had nothing to do with him, but my views would be put to the minister when he next surfaced. 'O.K.,' I said, 'then I'll get busy with my pen.' I wrote what I think could be described as 'the famous *Sunday Times* article'. I rough-drafted it, polished it and left it with Harold Evans, editor of the paper. It was to be edited, and held until I arrived home at Newcastle because I wanted time to think in the cold light of my train journey north, whether I should give it the final O.K. for publication. Before I had got back, Peter Shore had been ringing my home. Would I contact him? I rang him. I could not get through; his phone was out of order, so I published the article. It was a good article, I think. Important insomuch as I said for the first time publicly that I considered that unless one could be involved in policy decisions at regional level, then my sort of job could not be done. And effective too. I do not want to pretend that my gesture resulted in the changes which were made in the procedure for closing collieries. After all, a lot of discussion had taken place on this subject, and no-one more than Peter Shore had felt that changes had to be made. He appreciated the human problems. But I was the chap who actually talked to these people who were classed as problems. So my threat of resignation was not taken lightly. I meant it when I said that if Harrington closed, I would resign. There was no question about that. Dan Smith would leave the NEPC as the last cage at Harrington, in Cumberland, ascended the mine shaft. The only colliery scheduled for closure which was kept open in Britain apart from economic reasons, was Harrington. All the rest were closed according to plan. How much that was due to my efforts I will never know. What I do know is that the scant resources of popularity which clung to me evaporated. Shortly afterwards when Harold Wilson had taken the decision to appoint Fred Lee as Minister with Special Responsibility for the North, I was lunching with the Prime Minister and he remarked, jocularly but pointedly, 'There are a lot of pressures on me, but at least I have never threatened to resign.' The comment may have been apposite.

Anyhow, Harrington was kept open, albeit just for a matter of months. A fund was set up to keep collieries open and a consultative procedure established. I think it was a totally inadequate fund, and that was not what I was fighting for. I was intent on the right to consult and participate. I wanted industrial reorganisation to be planned, with the social and industrial consequences of any decisions which were to be made by governments or anyone else fully considered before decisions were reached.

It can be sensed, perhaps, that industry in Cumberland presented a headache to me. But over in North-East England the same sort of problem also existed. Way back in the thirties, the North-East Industrial Development Association had been established. It continued until after the Second World War. Its work, concerned with a depressed area, had been commendable. Before and after the war, Henry Daysh, pro-Vice-chancellor of the University of Newcastle, had played an important part in pinpointing the economic weakness of the area, especially of Cumberland. There was good will, earnest endeavour, some real action and much hot air. But unemployment still existed at a rate in excess of the national average. As an ex-dole boy, I was very conscious of this. I talked to Ted Short and Charles Grey, two of our regional M.P.'s. When Joe Eagles was in Newcastle I had discussed the problem with him. From these discussions had come the decision to form a body called the North-East Development Association. The concept of this 'ginger group' was discussed, argued, seminared and explored in depth, until eventually, under the aegis of the Lord Mayor, it had been established at a conference in the Old Town Hall in Newcastle.

This was one of the earliest occasions when people from the

North had gathered together and talked of the Three Rivers Country. It was one of the first times that Northerners had voiced the notion that there was such a thing as a region. The NEDC played its full part subsequently in creating the atmosphere of a region marching forward under the leadership of George Chetwynd and later Fred Dawson. But I had now to add impetus to this situation for I could not support the general governmental impression that our national economy was running at too rapid a rate, and that therefore half a million unemployed was to be considered a tolerable figure. The strategic ways of combating this assumption were, I felt, to instigate investigations by my NEDC in the areas of agriculture and education. In the second of these fields we were, I felt, a disadvantaged region. So my colleagues were launched into these projects, and the results were partially rewarding. Our report on non-urban problems was particularly pleasing; I felt that I could say with justification that we were, as a new organisation, looking to the well-being of people all over Northumberland, Durham, Cumberland, Westmorland and the North Riding. Education has always been a grey spot in our region. 'Get the bairns earning', has been a catch phrase. That must change. When it does, employment benefits will accrue, and I have no doubt that our relevant Planning Council report, when published, will have played its part.

All the more disappointing, then, to reflect that the Department of Education and Science never had a meeting with me, or with my chairmen-colleagues from other regions. Nor did the Ministry of Technology. In my view, these ministries were vitally important in shaping the quality of life in the regions. Yet their reaction to Planning Councils was lukewarm. They seemed to see their exclusive function as being job-trainers and job-providers. 'Worthy, but limited,' would be my end-of-term report on them.

But as time passed several ministries started to erode the power of the Department of Economic Affairs. The latter's national plan had not been received cordially, and personality difficulties at government level were beginning to show. I had my own share of these. I never quite got close enough to Harold Wilson, for instance. This was a pity, because Hugh Gaitskell and I had much in common. He had a soft spot in his heart for our deprivations in the north, and he was a 'big' man, generous and forbearing in debate. He found me something of an enigma because I was a pacifist and he was dedicated to German rearmament. But we were alike in our fighting qualities and herein lay our bond. He could tolerate a parochial provincial yapping round his heels, even at a time when Nye Bevan and he were battling about German rearmament. Not only was he willing to let me have the opportunity to develop my ideas on local government and regionalism, but he inconvenienced himself to give me those opportunities. Here was a man, it seemed to me, who had the kind of mind which, without demanding subservience, could on the one hand do battle, and on the other seek to maximize the contribution of individuals. I often think that herein lay his great strength. Most of my political friends were anti-Gaitskell. I wasn't. I was pro-Bevan, and this did not endear me to anybody. It seemed that one had either to be for or against a person. It was not considered reasonable for me to take part in an anti-nuclear march during the Labour conference and then be called upon to speak at the same conference on Labour's policy for local government. One either supped with the devil or one was the devil himself. One could not, it seemed, be independent or objective, because the times demanded an identity with left wing or right wing. George Brown had some of the same qualities as Gaitskell, though he was clearly a very different kind of person. At my home in Newcastle, we would discuss the problems of people in Park Road and Scotswood Road, the heartache of eviction, the enigma of architecture, and how one could effect the marriage of politician and professional in order to create a better society. I never had that kind of discussion with Harold Wilson. I regret this. I feel that basically I have more in common with Harold Wilson's thinking than I have had with that of George

Brown or Gaitskell. But despite the fact that I was chairman of the Northern Economic Planning Council there was very little effective dialogue between us. Certainly not as much as there was in pre-Planning Council days between myself and Harold Macmillan. And to some extent I was left with the feeling that as the DEA was disappearing in effectiveness, so Wilson washed his hands of it. And I always had the feeling that somewhere along the line the DEA would die.

I remember saying to George Brown when he was in Newcastle during a particularly difficult time for him, and when Harold Wilson was talking about economic miracles, that it does not always follow that one has to turn water into wine. It is a miracle sometimes if one turns wine into water. But I would wish to be fair to Harold Wilson. The pressures of office are great. I can only give it as my opinion that in matters of local government and regional development Gaitskell and Brown showed more understanding than Harold Wilson. I recall remarking to one of the officers in Transport House, when the Labour Party was swept out of power in local government, that it would not take much time and trouble to write to those people who had been leading local councils and thank them for the services they had rendered. But it was not done. It was felt that such a step would be identifying the Prime Minister with failure, and that was apparently of greater consequence than an acknowledgement of people having given of their best. In opposition, the Labour Party will have time to overhaul its public relations. Certainly, when Wilson inherited the DEA he nurtured it for only a short time before burying it. It would have been presumptuous of me to have expected some prior notice of this, even though I had given up a career in local politics to serve the DEA. But I did consider it somewhat ironic that, as a person who preached participation and consultation, I should find myself on the outside looking in. Or has this always been the lot of the man from the region?

I I

TIME OUT FOR CHAT

IT IS breakfast time on Sunday, the best time of the week. Relaxed, serene and chatty. Tea and toast, with a panatella to follow, make a man feel at peace with the world. One wants to hold on to such moments—to savour them to the full. Only one small shadow clouds the occasion. It is a typewritten sheet of paper lying close to the breakfast table. Flimsy, and inconsequential to the casual glance, it is in fact a slice of my life mortgaged to the future. In a few terse lines it carves up the week ahead, and timetables my every movement. It is demanding, it is ruthless, and it denies argument. It is my weekly schedule of engagements. A typical example lies in front of me now, for a week in January :

Monday.   Plane to London
 10.30 a.m. Royal Commission. Working lunch
 6 p.m.   Lord Peddie
 7 p.m.   Private engagement.

Tuesday
 10.30 a.m. Royal Commission
 1.15 p.m.   Television engagement
 4 p.m.   Business meeting
 7.30 p.m.   Meeting with ministers.

Wednesday
 10 a.m.   Desert Island Discs recording
 11.30 a.m. Business meeting
 6.45 p.m.   Festival Hall concert.

Thursday

9.25 a.m.	Plane from London to Teesside
11 a.m.	Teesside Airport committee
3 p.m.	Open Wiggins Teape Warehouse, Newcastle
6 p.m.	Computer Exhibition, Central Station.

Friday

9 a.m.	X-ray General Hospital
10 a.m.	Meeting at Wellbar House
11 a.m.	Press conference
Noon	Washington New Town
5 p.m.	Return to Newcastle.

An average sort of week, I suppose, although my secretary has written below it, 'You are overworking again.' But could one leave that piece of paper lying there and return to soothing Sunday? Could one, in fact, in this chapter, try to parallel the easy, reflective mood of a day off? The sort of mood in which ideas, opinions and memories crowd in one each other. This might be one way of revealing oneself. At least it should yield variety.

So it is Sunday. But I will not be attending church. My early choirboy days are a long way behind me. I now lack religious conviction. I believe that cities are what men make them, rather than 'without the Lord build a house his labour is in vain that builds it—'. My relations with clergymen have also been distant. In my teens, when I told a Wallsend parson that I had come to the conclusion that churchgoers were hypocrites, his response had been: 'So what? There is always room for one more.' On more than one occasion I have had to chide clergymen because I felt that their work for ordinary people was inadequate. Once I had eighty-three of them in front of me. I asked them why it was that folk wrote to me, at the rate of over one hundred letters a week. Youngsters, old people, lonely people and worried people flooded my desk with pleas for help. 'And,' I said, 'I'm not a Christian. You are. Why don't they write to you? Why me?' The answer was self-evident. They knew that I would do what I could for them, including the answering of their letters, in spite of having no secretarial staff at the town hall. 'But,' I added, 'I don't see that as being my job. It is yours. My job is to create the kind of community in which you, as believers, can operate.' I did my best to include a multi-religious centre in the city education precinct. It would have been easier to build a rocket-launching base!

To go out somewhere would be a pleasant way to spend a Sunday. But nowhere pretentious. Ada and I are not keen socialites. Cocktail parties leave me cold, and lunch in the Lord Mayor's parlour is a penance. These occasions bore me to death. I will not attend a Royal Garden Party. Indeed, after a 'brush' I had with Prince Philip, I may never receive an invitation!

Of course some formal occasions are acceptable. There was a pleasant dinner party given in London for Kosygin during his visit to Britain. Ada and I enjoyed that. I was due to fly to Moscow a fortnight later, so I gleaned some useful background information. Food and facts mix very well.

But really, my preference is for days out with down-to-earth, flesh-and-blood people. The Miners' Gala at Durham, although a smaller occasion than it once was, is festive and moving at the same time. A somewhat similar occasion which Ted Fletcher, Joe Eagles and others tried to restore to the streets of Newcastle was the May Day parade. Passing years had dampened enthusiasm for this event; our feeling was that the working class movement still needed to show its solidarity, and that if one organized occasions like a May Queen and a May Ball, the idea might attract youngsters. What was necessary was a personality to crown the Queen, and also draw the crowds. It seemed that Newcastle's Theatre Royal might prove the best bet for star names, and over the years I found myself in the wings, the dressing rooms and the bar soliciting grease-paint support.

On one occasion I cornered Tyrone Power, a real hero

of mine, who had recently played at the Abbey Theatre in
Dublin, and was starring in Shaw's 'Devil's Disciple' at
Newcastle. He wanted to know all about May Day—its
purpose, traditions and developmental background, and he
threw in his own verbal contributions from American trade-
union history. Eventually he said, 'Fine, I'll crown your May
Queen.' I called for him at the theatre on the Friday night.
Crowds swarmed round the stage door. We had a drink before
facing them, and again his talk was of Shaw, Sean O'Casey,
the problems of the Irish and the choices facing the world.
This was no playboy; I felt drawn to him. Moving out through
the silent auditorium he remarked, 'It was a marvellous perfor-
mance tonight. All those empty seats with people's bottoms on
them, and their minds concentrating on the stage.' Then we
were in narrow Shakespeare Street, with the crowds clamouring
for autographs and Tyrone obliging good-humouredly. At the
Oxford Galleries he charmed the dancers and captivated the
May Queen. On other occasions, stars like Pearl Carr and
Teddy Johnson also supported us. But surprise, surprise—I
could not get Frankie Vaughan to co-operate. Three or four
times I made the fifteen mile journey to Sunderland where he
was playing at the time. I did not even see or speak to him.

The May Day idea was a good one. The mediaeval apprentices and later the keelmen used to whoop it up in Newcastle
on regular occasions. Why not 20th century workers? But after
the driving spirits had turned to other things, the event lapsed.
One reason may have been that, in contrast to former times,
these affairs do not nowadays seem to throw up their local
characters as they once did. There is not the built-in catalyst
such as one tended to find in Tyneside politics in the twenties
and thirties, like David Harle, or, in the vernacular, Davey
Haall. I met Davey at the first indoor meeting I ever addressed.
It was an ILP affair at Hartford, a pit village in Northumberland. When I reached the hall there were 250 seats laid out
and an audience of three. I asked Davey if I should carry on.
'Why aye man,' he said. So I launched forth into European

problems, the Spanish War, and wasn't it a disgrace that the people of Hartford did not show more interest. At the end Davey turned to me. 'Why son,' he counselled, 'It's nee good playing waar wi' the buggers that's turned up—it's the ones that hasn't that deserves the hammer.' That was good for me. Another of my chairmen was the Ashington miner Charlie Cole. His stock remark was, 'I'm Cole from Ashington.' He was the first man I heard tell the story about the British going to Africa and telling the natives to look up to God. When they looked down again their land was gone. He chaired a meeting I addressed in the Haymarket Cinema in Newcastle in 1939. I spoke just before Jimmy Maxton. Warm, emotional and a dreamer, with a mass of hair tumbling down his back, Maxton impressed me greatly.

Mind you, we do have some local characters left. Not so long ago in the House of Commons Dame Irene Ward attacked me in an adjournment debate. She suggested that, in the interests of the North, I be transferred to the Southern Region. Twenty-six years earlier, when she had defeated Margaret Bondfield in an election at Wallsend, Dame Irene had actually come by my home and patted my young head. If she had only known! What a blow she might have struck for the North!

I am, of course, greatly interested in people—people of ideas. Whenever I was invited to address a University audience I would look forward to a valuable feedback. And I would enjoy talking privately to the tutors. I spent one stimulating evening with Sir John Cockcroft at Churchill College. Along with a group of students we talked until after two in the morning. When Sir John died I was asked if I would broadcast about him. 'But I only knew the man for twelve hours,' I protested. 'Maybe,' they said, 'but they were significant hours to him.'

Good company is also to be found at ministerial level. Barbara Castle, for instance, at the Ministry of Transport, impressed me with her efficiency and also with her charm. She did not get bogged down by detail, but insisted on looking at Britain's communications cobweb in relation to other aspects of life. In a sense she is, I suppose, like me, a lateral thinker. There is a commonly-held belief that it does not really matter who is minister—a government department will run itself anyhow. Barbara disproves this view. She quickly called together a group of people, including myself, to talk about the re-organization of transport. We met half a dozen times at the House of Commons, and her drive and ability impressed me. As a result, she attracted some outstanding civil servants to the Ministry of Transport, although it was rumoured that one or two of the old-stagers were not in complete agreement with her dynamism. As far as I was concerned, she was the one minister who, above all others, consulted with Economic Planning Councils. Stephen Swingler and Carmichael came north to talk to us, and the consultation was superb. When Barbara was succeeded by Richard Marsh, everything in the regional pipe-line was clogged up once more. It is an indication of the importance of ministerial priorities. Neither Frank Cousins nor Wedgwood Benn, during their association with the Ministry of Technology, seemed to be interested in our Planning Council either. And here we were in the North dependent on techno-logical advance for our economic wellbeing. I mentioned this to Jeremy Bray, but still nothing happened. When Wedgwood Benn speaks of the need to involve people in democracy I have to smile! Maybe he should take a lesson from Denis Howell. He seems to realise that a sports complex in Newcastle is of importance, and that sailing on the Derwent Reservoir is part of people's lives. George Brown also, of course, is a man of the people. When he left the Department of Economic Affairs, the heart went out of it; so did the lungs, the kidney and the liver. I began to feel that I was chairman of a balloon, and suspected that there was no future for Planning Councils. As long as George was in there pitching for the regions, morale was high. When he went, the bubble burst.

Roy Jenkins cannot, in my opinion, be summed up in such black and white terms. My first contact with him was when he wished to write a book on Hugh Gaitskell, after the latter's death. Ministerial commitments thwarted this meeting, but when he was established at the Ministry of Civil Aviation, I sensed that he was reaching out to the regions. When at the Home Office and when he moved to Number 11, he used to invite me on occasions to meet to hear from him about the general state of the economy, and of problems in the North and to solicit my views. He also used to venture north—speaking to him at the Gosforth Park Hotel, it was possible to sense his interest in grass-root opinion. Kindly and patient, he nevertheless remained something of an enigma to me. I could never tell quite what he was thinking. The private part of his mind was well-secured. From the mining community of Wales, he had made the difficult transition to the corridors of power. He was less at home on the balcony of a Durham hotel waving to pit-men than was George Brown. But he remains a man of great strength of purpose and integrity.

In a minor way, I have myself had to make this break from one culture to another. How successfully I have achieved it is for others to say. All I know is that it is no easy thing, and it has exposed me to criticism. This I have never resented. Much of my method of working is based on positive-type criticism. The whole process can be creative. Whether it has been planning a city, or encouraging a potential ballerina in Berwick, or pondering on whether a budding Sir Laurence should have to leave Morpeth to study at RADA, I have gone out of my way to stimulate discussion. One technique I have devised for accomplishing this has been the dinner party. Sometimes it would be in the Carlton Towers penthouse suite in London. But it might just as well be the timbered Red House on Newcastle quayside. Over a leisurely meal minds can work more easily and tongues operate more freely. Often I would brief head waiters to concentrate on the discussion rather than the dinner. If an important point was being made, the *vol au vent* should be discreetly delayed. If an awkward silence was evident, then the *vin rosé* was probably overdue. Sam Johnson managed best over a breakfast table, but I did quite well in the evening.

As a regional leader, I considered it part of my job to meet important people in this way. Yet, while I could thus gain counsel, and influence discussion, I never achieved a position of power. It is different for the regional politician abroad. Mayor Lindsay of New York, because of his office, may become a serious contender for the Presidency; Willy Brandt of Berlin has also 'made it' at national level; not so in England. I have had the ear of the U.K. power structure, but have not been accepted by it. Perhaps this is because I have resisted conformity. But I have at least talked to people like Alan Bullock, Lord Fulton, Lord Redcliffe Maud, Sir Frederic Seebohm and a host of others. We have rubbed minds and tossed around ideas. As a result I have gained immeasurably in understanding, and I may have been able to feed in a few pointers myself.

Just as the regional politician in Britain is less significant than his counterpart abroad, so our provincial press also plays a less distinctive role than does that of Germany, France, Italy or America. For example, there would be more newspaper inches devoted to keeping open Palmer's shipyard, even if the cost were a million pounds a year, than there would be to the alternative of opening a new polytechnic. There was more journalistic battling for Haverton Hill Shipyard than there has ever been for the concept of a University of Teesside. When Charles Clore decides to close Haverton Hill, financial subsidy comes within six months. Bully for Charlie! But does Teesside need Haverton, or does it need a university? Should not our regional press be asking questions of this sort? In my opinion they gear their stories too often to the industrial structure of the past. They fail to realize the objectives of the region in the long term. I believe that we need a new journal, something like the *New Stateman*, to supplement existing organs and to do the regional job as it needs to be done. A publication dealing with the arts, the economy, technology, sport and recreation, pitched at an intelligent level, would gain a viable readership. Though having said this, I would be the first to admit that our regional press has been more responsive to regional aspirations than have newspapers in cities like Birmingham and Sheffield. We have local talent too in our journalists. Eric Forster, of Newcastle *Evening Chronicle*, has been regional journalist of the year. And we have a rare critic in Tom Little. Even though he waxed bitter about Boris Brott, and took me to task for mentioning on a broadcast that I like to shut myself in a room, play orchestral records, and conduct them!

Harold Evans must have been one of the brightest editors that the *Northern Echo* ever had. He had a passion for the Northern Region and was always ready to fight for its causes. One can see the same pen at work currently in the *Sunday Times*. If ever Harold can dip it in regional ink he does so. Now, as editor of the *Northern Echo*, Don Evans carries on his predecessor's tradition.

What about the other regional media? In broadcasting and television I think that a man like Dick Kelly of the BBC has never had the opportunity to explore his potential fully. Perhaps, as a Geordie, he never got a fair crack of the whip. My opinion is that he would have made a first-rate regional controller; he has always had just the right amount of fire in his belly. The BBC has certainly done me proud. It has always been ready to allow me to present my region's case, especially on BBC1 and Radio 3. Not that local listeners have universally approved. I have often had critics accusing me of presenting a false picture of the North. 'Why Dan's Castle?' they would say. 'Why that big fellow again?' The answer from the BBC's point of view was that the big fellow had a big message, of national import, to send out to the country.

As for the other channel, I feel that some rationalization is required. As a member of the board of Tyne-Tees Television, I cannot see that there is a case for separate companies in Carlisle and on Tyneside. In fact at the Northern Economic Planning Council we have talked of a main northern broadcasting base at Manchester, with a powerful and real concentration on regional culture as exemplified by the Hallé, the Northern Sinfonia and Northern Opera. But that is some time in the future. Meanwhile Tyne-Tees Television, having recovered from the One O'Clock Show, is set for a comeback. It has a talented staff and a lot of bright ideas. As one of the most televisually exposed of people, I have a high regard for the medium. In a sense it usurps Parliament in its ability to propagate policies and ideologies.

Parliament! Now there's a thing. I have often been asked why I never offered myself as a candidate for the House of Commons. I have always had the same reservations about this as I had about going on the local council. Or about singing in the choir as a lad. If I was in the choir, I liked to sing the solo, then walk home. I did not want to know the choir. If, as a councillor, I spoke to a public meeting, I liked to get my message across, then go down amongst my audience and speak to the people about my subject. I could not chat about the weather or the football results or the Grand National. I wanted to know what made people tick. As a consequence, it would be fair to say that in my life as a councillor I was, in a personal sense, friendless. I had no part in the social life of the council. I must have been in Newcastle's Mansion House less than anyone. To be Lord Mayor would frighten me.

And similarly, when I considered whether I wanted to be an M.P., I used to think 'Well, I'm not the kind of man who is able to make that kind of contribution. I believe I know what the North needs. I believe that I am a man who can bring people together and work out ideas. It's in this direction that I would rather make my contribution.' On the other hand, many people in northern Labour Party constituencies continued to press me. If I had stood, I would have been unsatisfactory insomuch as I would have insisted on stirring things up. Even now I am not content to sit back and say, 'Well, Newcastle will not be a bad city. I'm 55 and why should I bother? I'll not see the end.' I have got to be telling people, as soon as they are going to sit down, to get up again. People basically do not like that, and I have seen this resentment reflected in their attitude to me. Their intensity of dislike is something I

have never understood. Because basically I have no personal
dislikes myself. I may dislike people's ideas, and I will say so.
But I do not hate any individual. I might oppose people's views.
And because I was trained on the soap box, and am a merciless
debater, I would go out of my way to destroy a man's ideas if
I believed they were wrong. So I would have been a rebel M.P.,
probably to the extent of out-Bevanising Nye. And I would
have been a poor back-bench man, because I cannot operate
unless I am singing the solo. So in the late forties I put Westminster out of my mind and decided that I was the provincial
who would stay at home and make regionalism work. I have
never regretted that decision.

This chapter started at breakfast time on a calm Sunday.
And now the shadows are creeping over the Leazes Moor, and
the city skyline is blurred. The lamp beside my piano casts a
glow round my sitting room walls. The family photographs
reflect back their warm timelessness. A ray of light strikes on
the framed parchment which declares that Thomas Daniel
Smith is a Doctor of Civil Law (Honorary) of the University
of Newcastle upon Tyne. Souvenirs of a dozen trips abroad glint
at me from occasional tables. My children drift in, and I sense
the basic security of the family unit. This is what politics and
regionalism and planning is all about. There are no problem
families. I have never yet come across a family where everyone
was a wrong 'un. Families suffer because of circumstances outside their control. My children have been the victims of other
people's opinion of me. People who have disliked me have taken
it out of my family. This has tormented me. And less enlightened people have been prone to remark to my kids, 'You'll
never be the person your father is.' Fortuitously, my wife and
my children now know the scene. They understand the situation. They have no social aspirations. Like me, they appreciate
a quiet domestic life.

And how about me, the problem father? Am I the confident
extrovert as the mass media would suggest? Far from it.
Although I have so often 'taken the chair,' 'led the meeting',

and 'pointed the way ahead', I have always felt inferior. I may have sparked off ideas, engendered enthusiasm, and manoeuvred policies, but in the end I have had to say, 'Now that is as far as I am able to go. Someone with more ability will have to take it from here.' And it is this basic insecurity which has prevented me from advancing my own claims as a person who might have contributed more at national level. So be it. The time for recollection and dreaming is over. Tomorrow is another day.

12

THE ROYAL COMMISSION

Wellbar House is a tall modern office block standing in Gallowgate, near the centre of Newcastle. It is the headquarters of the Northern Economic Planning Council—my base. Walking to it in the morning one is struck by the appropriateness of its situation. Directly opposite is an imposing brewery, all plate glass, patios and fountains, where Newcastle ale is produced in encouraging quantities. Up the road is St. James's Park, where Newcastle United play. Round the corner is the meteorological office, where Newcastle's weather is forecast. We are becoming so self-sufficient in the North that perhaps we should consider launching our own brand of nationalism. Herein lies a great delusion. It is not to cosy, inward-looking units that we in the regions should be attending. We should be lifting our eyes over our limited horizons, and attempting to visualize the togetherness which modern communications have ordained shall be our lot in the future.

Not that this is easy. Up in my pleasant, carpeted office in Wellbar House I have hammered away at a score of projects aimed at integrating aspects of life in the North and beyond. It might be the Steel Board with whom I consulted on the import of iron ore ; or the Water Resources Board ; or the Civic Trust. Then there were government departments to ask for their views, and gradually a vast jigsaw puzzle of ideas and statistics would emerge. It was clear that some of the pieces would not fit. Often it seemed that two or three puzzles were in the making, none of which had much relation to the others. This

was due in part to our inability as a Planning Council to communicate fully with the local planning authorities. I had an
excellent relationship with planning officers, but the machinery
for adequate consultation did not exist. This was strange,
because one of the perks of my job at the Northern Economic
Planning Council was the use of the diplomatic bag. I recall
being on holiday in Greece when an envelope was delivered to
me. It was from Roy Mason, consulting me on an announcement he proposed to make about a power station at Seaton
Carew. The Greek hotel janitor who was witness to this impressive diplomatic exercise, was clearly of the opinion that I
was of the James Bond set.

Yet here in Northern England we had not sufficiently good
communication channels to work our way through to the
production of a regional plan. When our second publication,
Regional Strategy, emerged from Wellbar House, it was really
a preface to a regional plan, whereas the regional plan itself
should have been the preface to a major injection into the
national plan. I could see that local government needed reforming in a drastic way. It needed reforming in a way which would
take account of the Treaty of Rome, and our likely entry into
Europe. I tried to chivvy the North into this sort of national
exercise, bringing together representatives of the CBI, the TUC
and my own Economic Planning Council, under the chairmanship of Sir James Steel. They did not know where to start. They
did not get down to any meaningful work. And now the North
is marching around like Long John Silver, except that we have
a patch over both eyes. We could be swept into Europe, having
by 1980 solved those problems which should have been solved
in 1940. There is a lot of work to be done.

Of course Economic Planning Councils are still young.
When they are replaced by democratically elected bodies
related to British needs in Europe, there will be possible an
exciting new phase of devolution and participation and their
role as generators of ideas will have been justified.

Yet my restless feeling in the mid-sixties was that more was necessary. This was why I welcomed the establishment of the Royal Commission on Local Government in England. It was why I agreed to become a member, and was pleased to be invited.

I found the experience to be a fascinating one. It took up a fair amount of my time over a span of three and a half years. I seemed to be in London as much as I was in Newcastle. But the experience of working with dedicated and scrupulously fair colleagues on an important issue was one I would not have missed. At the same time, I have reservations about the concept of Royal Commissions. I cannot think that the methods they employ are suited to dealing with urgent problems. Take, for instance, some of the Commissions which have been sitting in recent years: Fulton on the Civil Service, Goddard on the reform of trade unions and, currently, Crowther on the Constitution. The Cabinet may well have a strategic attitude to all of these, but the time which can be devoted to them by chairmen and members is limited. A fully-integrated programme is difficult to achieve; one needs a constant review of all aspects of our system in an age when events do not wait upon processes. Royal Commissions, unbiased and apolitical as they must be, rely too much upon experiences and methods of the past, instead of exploring the future. This means that society runs the risk of pressures for reform for the worst of reasons. A crime wave, for instance, may raise an instant judicial outcry for harsher penalties. Yet one surely cannot divorce the importance of a rejuvenated health service from an enlightened approach to the criminal. Again, Royal Commissions do not seem able to make much impression on the departmental empires of government. It was interesting to note that Richard Crossman was the minister who established the Royal Commission on Local Government. Then he was translated to the Ministry of Health, where he issued a green paper on the reform of the health services which came out strongly against local authority involvement. Now I cannot see how one can separate a person's health from his housing, his job, his journey to work, his leisure and his total environment. And I would suspect that Richard Crossman would also find it difficult to compartmentalize these attributes of an individual. Yet there was this apparent drawing back by him from our Commission's work as soon as we were outside his immediate orbit. And there was nothing we were able to do about it.

Of course our work was, in a sense, unique. It did not deal with one facet of life, but with the whole man from pre-birth to post-death. It attempted, so far as was possible within its terms of reference, to look into the future, bearing in mind the declining interest in local government. Its concern was with individuals. Local government had to be geared to a personal level, and those it was designed to serve had to be involved in it. They might be old-age pensioners, or handicapped children or I.Q. whizz kids—whoever they were, they had to be catered for. Their love might be the theatre, the open fell-land, the motor car or the brass band. So be it—they were bound to nudge local government in some respect. This was the Royal Commission's territory on which we were set loose to roam. I was no stranger to it. My map had been drawn up over a good many years.

Nevertheless, I felt that my contribution was small in comparison with that of my illustrious colleagues. Lord Redcliffe Maud was chairman of the Commission. A former civil servant, he had been with the Ministry of Fuel and Power, had served abroad, and was currently Master of a college. A man of great energy and ability, I found that he could play one on a line like a fish. I have myself felt the line running out or being pulled in. He hooked me anyhow. He was the right man for the job. The deputy chairman was John Bolton. Well-built and balding, he was the modern management man, and a good foil to John Maud. The latter knew local government inside out, whereas Bolton's experience was of the business world, as well as having served on a number of public bodies. It was interesting, sitting around that rectangular table, to observe the interplay between the two men. Lady Sharp, the sole woman on the Commission,

E

was a most enlightened civil servant. Britain owes her a great deal; it was her concern for participation in planning which has helped to revolutionize thinking in this field. She advocated our Royal Commission fifteen years earlier. Sir Francis Hill had a lifetime's experience of local government. Peter Mursell, bespectacled and from the lush southern region, contrasted with Vic Feather who knew about the difficulties of Selnec— South-East Lancashire and North Cheshire, as well as the business of the T.U.C. Jack Longland, well-known for his broadcasts, was Director of Education for Derbyshire and con- tributed expertly on national parks, sport and recreation. Reg Wallis was a politician, and a Labour Party organiser for the north-west. His comments were invariably shrewd and apposite. Hedley Marshall, former treasurer of Coventry, was an all- rounder, being a member of the Arts Council, and a person who helped to establish the Department of Local Government Affairs at the University of Birmingham. So, although I had my own well-developed ideas on the Commission's brief, these ideas stemmed only from experience. My colleagues were more knowledgeable. Nevertheless we shared a passionate desire to make local government mean something to individuals, and our comradeship was real and rewarding..

Lord Redcliffe Maud set a cracking pace. Generally there were two meetings a week, lasting from half-past ten to five o'clock. Lunch was taken on the premises and was usually spent in furthering discussion. So was our brief post-coffee consti- tutional round the block. And in this way we rattled through a great deal of material in the thirty months leading up to the signing of the final report at Gwydyr House in May, 1969. Sir Matthew Stephenson, the permanent secretary, was astute in his assessment of the sort of people who could work together harmoniously over a period of time. He also provided an excellent supporting staff who seemed to have an uncanny gift of being able to supply just the right map, chart, graph or statistic when required. These four people had the job of breaking-down Britain into provinces, city regions, sub-regions and local councils. They had to relate these to existing local authorities, water authorities, hospital boards, broadcasting regions and so on. Then they had to permutate the lot, postulating no provincial councils, but only metropolitan and unitary authorities. Communities were analysed, and their composition and aspirations examined. It was all efficient, and at the same time personal and sympathetic. When our other two assistants, the tea ladies, made their welcome appearances, they were not strangers from another world. Usually we had spent most of the day talking about people like them. It was that sort of Commission.

My contributions to discussions were centred on the thesis that there must be a correction of the regional imbalance which exists in Great Britain. If we could only devise a formula for producing balanced communities, then one could help not only our own people, but those of underdeveloped countries. Local government could not function adequately unless it had some control over industrial development. Economic strategy should be a function of the proposed provinces. I hammered away at this formula and, at the risk of boring my colleagues, did get their concurrence.

After all the talk and all the paper, was it worth it? I joined the Commission convinced that one of its final recommendations must concern regional government. At the end, I was still convinced, but felt that the case had not been proven. I was delighted when the Crowther Commission was established. It allowed me to put my signature to the Maud report, in spite of my reservations on its regional contents. Lord Crowther's constitutional investigations will highlight and complement our work, and put it in a European context. The delay is not a bad thing either. There should be caution in carrying out fundamental social changes ; one can so easily replace a functioning organisation by one which creaks. My feeling is that a proper assessment of the Maud Report will not be possible for twenty years. Social surgery works as slowly as that.

13

PETERLEE

I DO NOT claim to be a philosopher. But I have a lot of admiration for philosophers. From Plato to Russell their works have brought me pleasure and, I hope, some understanding. The pinpointing of problems, the analysis of dilemmas, the signposting of solutions—these are, when allied to the human situation, the stuff of life to me. Admittedly I view them in terms of my own experience and interests. And this means that the North of England and its people superimpose themselves on every page. We have so many problems in our region. We need great minds to work on them. One of the incongruities of the twentieth century is that of regional imbalance. The economic inequality between different parts of our tiny islands is an affront to society. Yet no one seems to know how to start on remedial measures with any certainty of success. My conviction is that it is not only to statisticians, economists or planners that we should look. There are so many historical and attitudinal factors involved. It is a total picture which is required, together with a dispassionate assessment, and integrated guide lines. And it is philosophers who can best supply these. Or at least it was until a century ago. Can modern philosophers think in global terms? Scientists and technologists can. Their work transcends frontiers. An epidemic in Pakistan can, in a matter of hours, be combatted by drugs and services from London. An earthquake can devastate an area in the Middle East, and next day bulldozers and cranes from Sheffield can be clearing the rubble. And throughout most of the world, man's life-span is being edged upwards, so that 80-year-olds are not now regarded as venerable oddities, but as senior citizens. For a person like myself, born in 1915 and nurtured on the thin pallor of old age in the thirties, this is a wonderful thing. It has also been a remarkable experience for me to visit Switzerland and Sweden and to see there, walking the streets, a generation of people not to be found in the feuding countries of Germany, France, Britain and Russia. I wrote a few lines about this 'ghost generation' haunting our own cities :

> Rarely in England will you ever see
> The sweet old couples, who appear to be
> Abounding in Switzerland. So well-dressed and neat,
> Real picture book characters in the street.
> With angelic smiles and the patience of age,
> Matured in peace, never missing a wage.
> Husbands have lived here ; missed two ghastly wars
> That wiped out manhood like cancerous sores.
> Ghosts walk in their places in countries around.
> War widows have memories ; no foot-treads to sound,
> Too often our old folk have fought and have lost,
> Our countries unknowingly paying the cost.

Just as war deprived Britain of a generation of men, so it prevented our creative concentration on the problems of regional imbalance. Now I cannot see our northern worries being resolved before 1980. And yet we think that we are advanced thinkers. Under four million of us clustering round the Pennines, out of an enormous world population which is increasing by leaps and bounds, and we cannot come to terms with our dilemma! In a situation where the corporate body presents apparently insoluble problems, what price the role of the individual?

All this has a direct link in my mind with enlightened local government, the science of management and the contribution of the philosopher. Life is so complex today that interdisciplinary approaches to it are necessary. Politicians, be they called Heath or Wilson, can try conscientiously and doggedly to improve the lot of regionally-disadvantaged people, and succeed only in making minimal progress. University dons can have a stab at solutions, and be wide of the mark. And with lack of success comes lack of understanding, and finally indifference. I have found this in the South-East of England, where most people have a bland unawareness of my own region's disadvantages. I have spoken to audiences there and asked them 'What advice have you for the North?' Their response has been trite. So I have asked a different question: 'What is really really meant by Science and Technology? How can they help to cancel out the minus sign that lies over my region?' And sometimes a feedback has come. 'The North can invent something,' I have been told. 'Or develop a drug, or build big ships.' But these are not the answers I want. Of course we can do these things. We are a gifted and industrious breed. But such objectives are limited. They do not begin to scratch the surface of the general quality of life in the North.

Then I have posed different questions. 'Suppose we look at Boston, USA, with over a dozen institutions of higher education within a five mile radius. Here is a vast investment in intellect. Is it not, then, significant that although Boston's education flourishes, its society is sick? Can it be that this academically advantaged part of the world has something to learn from the North Country?' And the answer is decidedly yes! Because my people understand the way that communities tick. They know about the arts and leisure and living together. Given the economy, we could create a virtual utopia. Given a ghost of a chance, we could set the world on fire with a qualitative contribution to the well-being of mankind. We could export ideas, and we could provide a pattern for similarly deprived regions and countries. The vision excited me. Could it be made reality?

One by one I started to analyse modern technologies. My staff and I worked assiduously on the objectives which

researchers had set for themselves. Our enthusiasm and excitement grew as the list lengthened. No more arthritis by 1985.
The majority of heart complaints conquered by 1990. Pain on
the way out. Hunger and malnutrition erased from the
dictionary. Not only could these achievements add quality to
our way of life in the North. They could also be exported and
benefit mankind. So where did we stand in all this? Was my
region pressing away at the frontiers of knowledge? The answer,
sadly, was not too encouraging. We had firms like ICI and
Procter and Gamble which were in the international league,
but there was also much apathy and even suspicion of modern
technology. This I felt to be wrong. We should surely embrace
the new technology rather than turn our backs on it. Indeed
the very tools which, carelessly used, threaten individualism,
can in their right use lift man from much of the serfdom im-
posed by their absence in the past. The great advances in communications, for example, can remove the perils of secrecy, and
the pettiness associated with national frontiers. There can be
a release of the spirit.

I was able to float these ideas at a conference on Space and
Magnitude at Brighton, to an audience of distinguished
architects, planners, academics and civil servants. I was an
amateur. Yet I was assured that my contribution exposed the
nakedness of the professionals. They talked around my ideas
and showed awareness, but their thinking was, it seemed to me,
too narrow—too disciplined. A dash of vision would have
helped. For my part, I found a structure developing in my own
mind. Maybe all the chipping away which I was doing at the
expense of other people's complacency was paying off—for me
at least. And I tried to incorporate this structure in *The
Challenge of the Changing North*, where, for the first time,
there was a statement of objectives in which science and technology were to be priority considerations in the correction of
our region's imbalance. Jeremy Bray responded encouragingly.
Although he and I never got on together too well, he seemed
to be on my wavelength in this venture. He did, however, want

to ensure that any results and benefits accrued to Teesside.
My desire was to see that the north as a whole was the winner.
So there was this early difference between us, and as he was
a junior minister at that time, and a keen, able man, I was
worried by our failure to see eye to eye.

Then one day in 1967 Lord Wynne-Jones came along from
the University of Newcastle to see me at home. 'Dan', he said,
'I have been thinking about the role in the region of science
and technology, and it has occurred to me that there is something of a parallel situation in North Carolina. There the
economy is in decline, with the basic products of cotton and
tobacco being less in demand. Senator Hodges, State Governor
of North Carolina, has for five or six years been mounting a
rescue operation. I would like', continued Wynne-Jones, 'to
introduce you to Maurice Goldsmith, an official of the Science
of Science Foundation in London. His organization includes
many of the finest scientific minds in this country, and we could
find out if North Carolina is likely to pay off.'

The suggestion was a good one. Along with one of the best
brains in Britain, A. V. Williams, general manager of Peterlee,
the new town in County Durham, Lord Wynne-Jones and I
met Maurice Goldsmith. It was a meeting of mixed fortunes.
Wynne-Jones was, of course, an eminent professor of chemistry ;
but his concept of the science campus was in need of serious
modification if it was to develop. Maurice Goldsmith was a
different kettle of fish. A man of deep understanding and firm
conviction, his mind was alerted as I spilled out my ideas.
Dark-haired and personable, he talked in romantic terms about
the contribution which research and development could make
to society. His was a think-tank approach. Immediately, he set
about making it possible for me to meet his colleagues, and
searched for a formula which would link the Science of Science
Foundation with our northern schemes. Here, I felt, was a man
who was reaching out towards the efficient planning of resources
in the cause of human advancement.

I sensed that things were moving. Hurriedly, A. V. Williams

drafted a report for me to submit to Harold Wilson and other
Ministers I knew. Fortuitously I also let Ted Heath and Lord
Hailsham be privy to my thinking. The report summarized my
conclusions on the part which I envisaged that science and
technology would play in advancing the quality of life in the
North. It also included Goldsmith's notion of how this pattern
could be transferred to other regions. A series of discussions
took place, and at an early stage it became clear that the arts
and humanities had to be an integral part of the project. This
was to be more than an exercise in efficiency. It was to be an
example of excellence. We were groping towards an exercise
in participation and involvement which would permit scientists, dramatists, technologists, poets, engineers, artists, broad-
casters and sculptors to rub shoulders in a creative working
situation.

At this point a further stroke of good luck came my way.
Professor Flowers came north to inaugurate the joint computer
project between the Universities of Durham and Newcastle.
I saw my opportunity, and went out coldly and deliberately
to get at IBM. John Hargreaves, director of public affairs for
IBM was at the inauguration. A man of sensitivity, I could see
that he reacted positively to my outline of the things we were
about, and my hint that his mammoth company might care to
be involved. The image of the impersonal whizz-kid computer
man was not upheld in Hargreaves. As an IBM employee he
had said in his Ramsey Muir Memorial Lecture at Nottingham
University, 'There are other criteria besides efficiency and the
public good. Efficiency too often is seen as an end in itself,
whereas it may be the last and least important ingredient in our
affairs, especially if a degree of inefficiency safeguards individual
happiness. In the drive for efficiency, the end may be lost in the
means, and we may too easily forget in the search for the public
good that housing, education and employment are not
"things"—but individuals.' This sounded like my sort of man!
I invited him, along with the regional manager for IBM, to
visit Peterlee, of whose development corporation I was chair-

man. It seemed to me that, as a new town, nestling comfortably
in the region, and strategically placed in relation to universities
and industry, Peterlee might be the soil in which we could plant
our new hybrid. There we stood, looking out over the soft-grey,
growing town. It had a location of great beauty. Victor
Pasmore's hands had nurtured it over the years. His buildings
flowed in easy lines over the landscape. He did not plan so
much as caress a site. I could see that my companions were
impressed. The sun was working overtime, Castle Eden Dene
looked all that a nature reserve should, and the Argus Butterfly,
a pub which perpetuates the name of a rare butterfly found in
the Dene, was there to receive us. While our thoughts were of
the future, we were also conscious of the history of the area.
Peterlee was a well-balanced town. It captivated us that day.
It meant that IBM were ready to carry their thinking further,
and several of their executives paid visits to the town. The next
step was to visit America, to look at the North Carolina scheme
and to talk to IBM over there. The company's French president
received us kindly. He had the brain of a scholar, the shrewd-
ness of a business executive, and the strategic approach of a
politician. In principle, there was agreement that IBM would
invest money and men in the Peterlee project. We went to
North Carolina and saw the creative work being undertaken
there. It was impressive, but I was convinced that our own
schemes were more exciting. We also saw something of New
York, and there, strangely, echoes of Northern England
abounded. On the programme of the New York Symphony
Orchestra was the name of Boris Brott. Only eighteenth in the
list of conductors admittedly, but evidence that when we chose
him as conductor of our Northern Sinfonia Orchestra we had
been right. In the Lincoln Centre was the work of Henry
Moore. He and I had joined forces in a bid for Yorkshire
Television. Later, Newcastle bought a piece of his sculpture
at a comparatively knock-down price. Maybe we were not
entirely out on a limb in the Three Rivers Country!

I returned to England jubilantly. The possibility was that

IBM would inject several million pounds in the Peterlee operation, and establish a nucleus of highly-qualified men whose work would be to investigate the problems of the individual in society and in relation to his total environment. We were, as a region, embarking on a new venture, and it was essential that we should grasp its import. I had help from Vice-Chancellor Bosanquet and his successor Henry Miller, at the University of Newcastle, and from Vice-Chancellor Christopherson of Durham University. They enabled me to communicate with heads of certain faculties. Professor Page, in charge of the computing laboratory at the University, was also a tower of strength. Principals of polytechnics and institutes of further education throughout the area were consulted, and local authority officers briefed. I was heartened by the feedback I received. County Durham went on record as supporters of the project, and my colleagues at Wellbar House worked strenuously on the processing of the many suggestions and comments which flooded in.

Meanwhile, our dialogue with the Labour government continued. Fred Lee, who was minister with special responsibility for the North, arranged a meeting between myself and several cabinet ministers. The subject was whether the Peterlee project, as a unique experiment, would merit government support. Jeremy Bray was there, and we had a showdown. Although a kindly man I thought he had blind spots, and that Peterlee was one of them. He lost that day. We got government support. I do not think that all the ministers present at the meeting understood what it was all about, but they nodded their heads and gave the green light. Jeremy Bray resigned that week. He seemed to be a sad man and I felt sorry for him. I think that maybe the Peterlee defeat was partially responsible for his decision to go.

I was delighted that things were shaping well for the North. I held a press conference to spread the good news, and to announce the formation of a Regional Science Committee to co-ordinate local efforts in this field. What a let-down that

press conference turned out to be! There was a mood of scepti-
cism amongst the reporters. Alex Glasgow of the BBC hinted
that all this talk of science and technology was O.K. for egg-
heads, but what did it mean to the ordinary chap in the pub
at Peterlee? My response was that I met people in the pub at
Peterlee, and the proposed development meant a great deal to
them, and would mean considerably more to their children and
grandchildren. But cynicism was abroad that day. The press
boys seemed to expect miracles, and I was a bit short-tempered.
Never mind—that was in March 1969, and by October of that
year we had twenty Ph.D.'s installed in a new building at
Peterlee. The credibility gap did not exist on our side. From
investment to construction there was never a hitch. From notion
to implementation no impediment occurred. And this was in
part due to a lot of co-operation from the canny, reticent local
councillors at Easington, in whose area we were. We talked a lot
together, and they reached for the stars. Their confidence was
soon justified. When industry knew of the idea, they started
enquiring about the possibility of moving to Peterlee. The spin-
off was starting, albeit slowly.

I had problems with the Regional Science Committee.
Membership was agreed on, but it was essential that the right
chairman be found. Lord Wynne-Jones felt that he should have
the post. I disagreed. Instinctively I would have liked to
nominate him, for I have a high regard for him, as I had
for the late Lady Wynne-Jones. I thought he was not the man
for the job. Together with Henry Miller and A. V. Williams,
I suggested Dr. Bosworth, with Professor Musgrave of Durham
as vice-chairman. At the Committee's first meeting, Bosworth
was quite brilliant. He seemed to know just where he was
heading. But only time will tell. I am, in fact, apprehensive of
the future of the Science Committee.

I recognised that the growing team of Peterlee converts
would not be able to commute across the Atlantic as frequently
as was desirable during the early stages of the new project.
What we needed was a front-man to speak for us in the States,

and to feed information to us. So I said to Eddie Nixon, who was in charge of IBM in Britain, a man who had worked himself up from nothing to be the head of that pretty tough, if enlightened commercial organisation: 'Look, I want to talk to Lord Cromer.' He was the chairman of IBM and had been a fairly outspoken critic of the Labour movement when he was governor of the Bank of England. Nixon arranged that I should meet him, and we had a long afternoon discussion with him and John Fairclough. What I said to Cromer was, 'I want someone who has international reputation to go to America, to be known in America, to open doors in America and at the same time to be excited by our Peterlee project. He must be a man who doesn't feel that coming up North is in any way a chore.' Lord Cromer thought and then said, 'You want to meet the man who was the former British ambassador to America, Sir Patrick Dean.' My response was, 'Right, that's a fair assignment. Do you know him?' 'Frankly no,' replied Cromer, 'I've met him, but I don't know him. However, what I will do is write him a letter and send you a copy.' Thus he made it possible for me to meet Sir Patrick Dean. Off I went, knowing that by this time he had become a director of two or three companies in Europe, America and Britain. I met him in London. I succeeded in firing his imagination on Peterlee. He said, 'I've got a limited amount of time. I go to America four times a year. I go to Europe about the same number of times. But what can I do?' I convinced him that there was a job to be done, and outlined broadly what I saw this job to be. I succeeded in getting him signed on to the Peterlee team, and he accepted our assignment for a modest fee. Things were really beginning to move.

I talked to other people too. Dr. Bruce Archer of the Royal College of Art was excited by our project and may have much to contribute in the future. When Jennie Lee and Denis Howell were ministers I also brought them into discussions. Charles Curran and Arthur Clifford talked around the proposed television workshop, along with Frank Price, whom I remembered from the days when he brought theatre-in-the-round to New-castle. My past was catching up on me in a pleasant way, and I was grateful for the diversity of interests which had always been part of my make-up.

Where do we stand now? Well, we started with the nagging problems of the North. We snatched at an idealistic remedy, worried away at it, developed a concept, sold it to people of influence, and now have bricks, mortar and brains as the beginning of the realisation of our object. Out of a mass of specialisations, we believe that we can engender a climate of research which will feed from our region a stream of creative ideas to the ultimate benefit of mankind. It may sound like a philosopher's dream. As I hinted at the beginning of this chapter, it is meant to be!

14

THE ONES THAT GOT AWAY

TO WRITE an account of one's public life is presumptuous. Why should anyone want to read about another person's endeavours and triumphs and frustrations? Each of us has enough of his own to be getting on with. Only in the sense that my ideas and aspirations have been, for better or for worse, conceived on behalf of a large number of individuals, can I claim some excuse for this book. It is intended as a means of communication. It also aims to put the record straight, so that I can be judged objectively by results, rather than by rumour. Nobody asked me to work hard in public life; I would like people to understand my motivation. In order to round off the picture then, it is necessary that I pinpoint a few failures, because failure is a built-in ingredient of everyone's career, and I have had my share of it. In the first place, there have been several ideas which I have cherished over the years, and which have come to nothing.

For example, between 1958 and 1962 I felt that the children who were growing up in the Northern region should have some back-up to their education through a regional zoological society. I had discussed this with a number of people and eventually concluded that Desmond Morris, author of *The Naked Ape*, would be a useful authority with whom to talk. I spent some time studying what he had written and then went to Regent's Park where, at the Headquarters of the Zoological Society, I met him with Mischa Black. We talked about costs, and possibilities, and the educational advantages of such a proposal

137

to the North, and I was assured that it could be a winner. I
went through all the procedures that I had done with the Arts
and similar ventures, but somehow I could not get this one off
the ground. Too many people had the concept of a zoo, rather
than an educational enrichment of the region. Why do we
have to label things? Is there some basic lack of security which
forces us to compartmentalize our thinking? I saw the proposal
as one antidote to the region's educational deficiencies. We will
never create the equivalent of the British Museum in the North,
nor can we transfer the Tate Gallery to Tyneside. But we can
at least do something to build up our own centres of excellence,
and our primary sources of reference. Our youngsters deserve
this sort of effort.

The frustrations which I encountered over the affair must
have influenced my hobbies at the time, for I remember
spending some time in the Lake District carving from wood a
montage of animal shapes which I visualized as an exercise in
movement, as one would envisage a mobile. I seem to have mis-
laid it, although it was one piece of carving that I felt rather
proud of. Honesty forces me to admit, and suspicion prompts
me to report that my wife did not accord it equal praise. Back
in the early sixties I felt that Brancepeth in County Durham was
the right place for the zoological society. I saw this as a mid-
regional site, convenient for our universities, colleges and schools
so that students and children could regularly investigate at first
hand the excitements of evolution and environment. But although I put the operation through what I think I can now
call 'the process', there was no positive response. I can appreciate, of course, that people had probably begun to think by this
time, 'God, is there no limit to what has got to be done in the
North?' And the arguments that can be advanced in support of
chimpanzees and yaks as contributors to regional well-being
tend to be limited.

Another non-starter which I would have dearly liked to see
in operation was a transport museum. Our region is intimately
associated with the development of railways and shipping. It

has contributed much expertise and know-how in this field. How appropriate it would have been to centralize the nation's record of transport development in George Stephenson countryside. How worthwhile it would have been also, to have added to the new terminal buildings at Newcastle Airport a facsimile of the aeronautical museum in Switzerland. It would have been a commercial winner, and might have evolved into a space repository, with a lively link to pioneering departments in our polytechnics. I could see youngsters wondering at early water-borne transport on the Nile, pondering over the arrogant beauty of the *Mauretania*, and involving themselves in simulation techniques in a link trainer. In other words, this would have been a living, moving museum, using the airport's restaurant facilities all the year round, and providing a point of attraction. I can never get over the fact that if a new type of 'plane touches down at Newcastle on a Sunday, crowds will go to see it. The same thing happens with giant ships on the Tyne. We are a proud and interested lot of folk in the North. We tend to be let down by those who plan for us. Their imagination does not match our aspirations.

So the transport museum never got off the ground. As some small compensation we did succeed in preserving the *Turbinia*, which is in Newcastle's Exhibition Park. But even that nearly went 'down the river'. I remember Nobby Bell, the lively city councillor, playing a part in this salvage job. The *Turbinia* was at that time in two halves in widely-separated parts of the country. In the city council this matter was raised, and it was suggested that we should bring the halves together and house them on Tyneside. After all, the *Turbinia* was the famous ship which had enabled Charles Parsons to introduce the steam turbine to an astonished world. But councillors were in a pinchpenny mood. I remember Nobby Bell saying, 'Well, we can always bridge the gap with Cadbury's Snack'. It was beautifully said and it was, at the same time, such an appropriate throwaway line. One felt like adding, 'for God's sake, if we can't see the importance of this, we might as well bridge the gap with

Cadbury's Snack.' It put our petty discussion in the right
perspective.

Our new Civic Centre in Newcastle is a source of pride to me.
Anyone journeying on the A1 cannot fail to notice it, jutting
over St. Thomas' Church, with the Tyne God spreadeagled
over its south-facing wall, and the fountains playing. In the
evening, people stroll along the floodlit terraces for the enjoyment which they are afforded by the pleasant vistas. This is the
exciting situation which architecture can produce. For a public
representative like myself it is the only reward that one could
ask for.

But we had our troubles. For instance, there is a magnificent
banqueting hall incorporated in the Centre. Analogous to the
baronial halls of early Northumbria, it blends dignity with
grace. It cries out for appropriate furnishings. But what have
we got? Cutlery and crockery appropriate to a 1930 snack bar.
Condiments straight out of a motorway pull-in. Because of
financial shortsightedness, an important qualitative element
has been sacrificed. And, sadly, it is shortcomings which get
attention, rather than rightness and fitness.

This brings me back to the point which I attempted to make
earlier ; that the present must be prepared to pay for the future.
We cannot buck the issue. That is why Pasmore was let loose
in the Civic Centre's Rates Hall. The provocative result was
planned intentionally and responsibly. I wanted people to go
in there, albeit reluctantly, to pay their rates, and to come face
to face with Pasmore's abstract art. I willed them to react
actively. As they fingered their cheque books or opened their
purses, I longed for them to snarl, 'This is the end.' Not because
I am a masochist, but because I believe that this is what the
relationship between the artist and the individual is all about.
People have eventually got to face the question of what
priorities they consider it worthwhile paying for. Democracy
may in this way become reconciled to its role as patron of the
Arts. Certainly those of us concerned with the Newcastle Civic
Centre were at pains to see that finance was available to

permit the commissioning of works of art for it. More so, I suspect, than did many elected bodies in Europe. In fact, the building is in many respects an art gallery, which has been visited by over 50,000 people. How many will have passed through our city Laing Art Gallery in the same period? Many people in fact shy away from such galleries. The Arts are for the people, of the people, and must be constantly communicating with the people. We have not yet achieved this in the North, but we are building up a credit balance.

Not so with another aspect of the Civic Centre which I fought for. This related to a link which I wanted to see between the Centre's registry office and the University Church of St. Thomas. These buildings almost adjoin on the same parkland site, within shadow length of each other. They sit easily together and relations between cloth and laity are good. Why not, I thought, symbolise this link by an architectural bond? The proposed marriage room was merely an attractive, purpose-designed suite of offices at the end of a corridor. It was designed to serve those couples who, for whatever reason, do not wish to have a church wedding. Surely it would be possible to express, on that unique site, the essence of the bond of marriage. In my mind's eye I saw Barbara Hepworth and George Kenyon working on this theme, but I could not convince my colleagues. The project has not yet come to fruition. It would be easier, of course, to fight these battles if my idea of a City Arts Director had been implemented back in the early sixties.

It was my contention that all cities needed a principal officer responsible for the Arts. They were not be restricted by com- mittee procedure which attempts to separate libraries from art galleries and so on. Rather should they have the general brief of stimulating creativity, and resisting the mediocre, in all aspects of a city's life. I would, for example, have expected an Arts Director in Newcastle to tackle an engineer about a proposed bridge, or a by-pass, or a street sign. His concern would be with these things, rather than booking the London Philharmonic Orchestra for a specific date. He would, in my

estimation, have been a sensitive man with his finger on the
City's aesthetic pulse. The Chairman of the Establishment
Committee in Newcastle listened to these ideas, and eventually
agreed to the appointment of an officer at £2,000 a year. But
this did not seem to me to be 'on'. We needed a man of sufficient calibre to merit a much higher salary. So the venture was
still-born, as was a similar idea which I advanced for a City
Sports and Recreation Officer. The Royal Commission makes
reference to some of those ideas in a section of the Arts, though
I have some reservations on many of its recommendations.

Much of my work has been centred on young people. Holly
Avenue and Portugal Place were fine for me, but I want something different for our present young generation. More bricks
and mortar I have been able, perhaps, to help them with. My
generation has been fair in this respect. It has done its duty.
But in terms of idealism and ethical standards, I have doubts.
I am concerned that in such respects we may be losing an
opportunity. Today a tremendous revolution in music and
clothes and colour and thinking has been telescoped into half
a decade. Young people of the 'pop' generation grow up so
rapidly nowadays, whereas it took me 20 years to come through
the slaughter houses, the schools, the slums, the poverty, the
strikes and the unemployment. Today there are not as many
soul-destroying shoals on which emotional and aesthetic development can become stranded. It is full steam ahead. The things
that perturb our youngsters are the intangibles. When I go
down Carnaby Street now, I find it delightful. I think 'Thank
the Lord.' There's colour; there's design; there's texture;
there's material; there are shirts that are fluffy and frilly, and
there are gay suits and exotic ties and lovely colours. This is
good. It's stimulating. It's a rebellion, in a sense. It's like
cocking a snook at my own generation's conventions of dark
suits, and trouser turnups, and short back and sides once a
fortnight. And leading the rebellion are the more intellectually
privileged; the kids who go on into further education, up to the
university. I say privileged, because it's not all just hard work.

I think the luck of the draw as to what kind of brains you happen to have fixed in your skull at the beginning makes a difference.

But then we have to recall that these youngsters are also grappling with the bomb. This is an offstage problem which was never posed to us. War is now an instrument of total destruction. It can be atomic energy for peace, or atomic energy for war; but atomic energy for war means the end of of the world. There is no long-term future for democracy possible if politicians behave in the future as they have so often behaved in the past. I think that I can sense why some thoughtful youngsters attempt to escape these insoluble problems of the world by resorting to drugs. We will no more cure drugs by legislation than we will cure crime by putting people in prison for longer terms. We have to acknowledge the tragedy of the confirmed drug-taker, in New York if you like, lying about the streets, without a home. While at the other end of the scale we have the intellectual reaching for the sky. The vast mass of young people in the middle are still happy with a pint of brown ale. They're happy with an intellectual pint of brown ale.

There is no doubt in my mind that the lack of purpose, the restlessness and the brown ale mentality of many of our youngsters can be blamed on the failure of the church to render unto God the things that are God's. Youngsters don't feel that the Church is in there, fighting. Maybe it is wakening up a little. A couple of bishops came out against the 1970 South African cricket tour. One even said, 'Let's hope it rains'. Then we wouldn't have to face the problem.

And so our kids look for new idols; they worship graven images. I think they saw in the Beatles and the Rolling Stones gods ready-made to bow down to. And mammon honoured them. The Establishment gave the MBE to the Beatles for their doubtful contributions to society. The Rolling Stones blotted their copy-book too early, or they might have been in the House of Lords by now. It all follows a pattern; the Beatles were popular, so we gave them honours. Never mind what they did or what they represented. Whether they were good as an example to youngsters, or men of character. If they're a hit, and they help the export drive, then they're 'in'. Well, all right, but how wrong then to turn on youngsters and say, 'You are drug-takers, you read pornographic literature, you are dissolute.' We as a society have set the pace and consecrated the standards. The role of politicians should not be, in my opinion, to go around handing out OBEs but to give the young generation a vision. They must try to harness the tremendous energy of teenagers to the advance of society. When Julie Felix or Donovan sing 'Where have all the flowers gone?' or 'When will we ever learn?', this is good. One feels stirred, as one did when Marlene Dietrich charmed us with her own version.

But this searching for the good, this inarticulate yearning for a set of ideals, arouses a strictly limited response in the politician. He is not leading towards any promised land. He is trying to interest people in the balance of payments and in prices and incomes—rather like the money-changers in the Temple. Politicians help to create idols. They help to perpetuate a situation where it is almost inevitable that drug-taking will flourish. There is no picture of the future of the sort which politicians, philosophers and authors were able to write and speak about in my youth. I think this is bad unless somewhere around the corner is a Bernard Shaw, or a Keir Hardy.

Although I believe that man can create a city, he can create only buildings and environment. He can create educational structures that help people to move forward and to think about their problems. But in the end there must be some vision of a promised land. I do not see this promised land. If all our energy, our advance in terms of design and colour, of curtains and houses and cars, of all the things that make life today so different from the drab nowhere of Portugal Place—if all this is to have significance, then we must have inspirers to point the way. We must somehow bridge the credibility gap between our leaders and our people. There is hope in seeing young people concerning themselves with organisations like Save the Children and the Oxfam movement. Here is the right kind of leadership in emergence. But to them honour? No. To the Beatles, yes. To Georgie Best, yes. But to people in general, who give devoted and dedicated service to the world, no. We are in many respects philosophically bankrupt. If I could give a tentative hint as to one goal we might set ourselves, it would be creation of a new Europe. The societies that were Roman, and Greek, the great traditions such as opera in Germany and freedom in Britain, if these and all other age-old and well-tried qualities of the nations were properly organised in democratic form, linked by the forward thinkers of our technological age, there could emerge a decisive contribution towards solving some of the problems which stalk the Afro-Asian areas. The concept of a Europe united for liberty and idealism could lift the eyes of our young people.

And the people of the North will have to lift their eyes also. Our besetting sin of parochialism, and living for the day, could cost us dear. In particular we must try to shed insular loyalties and rid ourselves of long-standing prejudices. If, for instance, one talks about Newcastle as the regional capital, does this in fact imply the relegation of Wearside and Teesside to obscurity? Does it mean that their acceptance of Newcastle as a regional capital is in any way a reflection on their own future growth? I think not. I think the opportunities to create a greater Teesside are not adversely affected by anything that Newcastle does. What will lead to a greater Teesside is the quality of thinking that goes into its making. So can we consider the question of the 'City base' and its problems?

The first would be those concerned with the provision of services. As an example we can take the recent proposal to develop an airport at Sunderland. Sunderland Council have been parochial for the past two or three years and there has for longer than this been an ongoing argument about whether the town should make any contribution to regional bodies, because it does not see benefits accruing directly. 'O.K.,' says the council, 'Then let us go it alone on our airport, and concentrate

on charter flights.' There must, of course, be a large investment
in order to improve the runway. Has any thought been given
to the fact that by 1972 Sunderland will be only twenty minutes
from Newcastle Airport? Equally, with Teesside Airport, a jet
service has been inaugurated to fly a thrice-daily schedule to
London. If it doesn't pay, it comes off. If one looks at the figures
for Teesside Airport, the number of people who flew in March
1970 from there was only about 4,000. Even if one were to
multiply this by 12 and treble it, it would still total only
140,000. This is not viable. The first thing we must determine
is how far each particular part of the region can make a contribution to the facilities and services that the region as a whole
needs. This demands big thinking, not only in staking a claim
for what each constituent community wants, but even bigger
thinking for the things which they can do without. These two
points are critical in politics. In the main, one is lucky to get
either of them.

One seldom meets the politician who is prepared to say, 'In
my view, we don't need an airport.' So basically I would want
to say that, in terms of communications, there is no future for
the Tyne as a major Euro-port. And here I would be talking
in European terms. Likewise there is no future for a major airport viewed in Tees terms, and again in a European context.
There is, however, future for a European airport on Tyneside,
because it has a catchment area that can make it a commercial
success. Similarly, we would encourage the development of
Teesport as one of the great petrol, chemical and steel ports of
Europe. That poses, of course, another question. How far in the
development of the airport at Newcastle would one be able
to cope with the noise problems of tomorrow's air services?
And how far can one envisage coping with the problems of
pollution that the industrial complex on Teesside will inevitably
create? My own view is that the Teesside monster will extort
from the community a price which will be incompatible with
the quality of life demanded by individuals in the seventies and
eighties. Therefore, the settlement pattern of Teesside must be

considered within a wider context. There must be questions asked about the optimum distance that one should live from work, in order to escape from atmospheric and other forms of pollution. We are really only toying with this dilemma at the moment.

The same goes for the exploitation of potash in the National Park in the North Riding at Whitby. This is an industrial prize, but a qualitative loss ; it is ruthless despoliation of the landscape. At the moment, I doubt very much whether society is willing to face the critical question of how great a price we have to pay for the development of our industrial system. I am, of course, arguing that urban separation from such forms of industrial development needs entirely different thinking. I really cannot think that it is possible to imagine that for the next twenty, thirty or forty years our ability to control pollution of different forms will match the degree of tolerance demanded by informed and enlightened citizens.

So we must, in the North, pay particular attention to the noise factor which will be inherent in the development of Newcastle Airport. At the moment there is a limited Trident service and that involves a lot of noise for a lot of people. It adds its strident voice at the same time as it makes its contribution to increasing prosperity. To these environmental features we have to ally the region's economics. If the Tyne is not going to be a European port, and the Tees is, what are the consequences for our community of those decisions? How many Tyneside politicians will look on the Tyne as a shipbuilding area, and how many as a river for recreation? How many politicians on Teesside will be far-sighted enough to write-off Teesside Airport as a major airport, as I myself would say it should be? And will there be consideration of the future developments of transport which may make air travel within our country, as distinct from between countries, almost obsolete?

But let us return for a final look at Newcastle. We now know that it will not be long before this city will become a unique example of modern planning and thinking ; it may be another ten years, or, if one takes a pessimistic view, twenty years. By that time it will have taken some thirty years, from the period of its conception, for the new Newcastle to rise from the old. It will have taken, in my own personal terms, a span of years dating from being a relatively old young man to being a relatively young old man. So we ought to stir ourselves now about the ideas I am floating, if we want to ensure that by the year 2000 something has been done. Newcastle must remain on the progressive wave, and so must the whole region. Everyone will have his own concept of future developments. My ideas for the city would embrace the growth of a second major education precinct, the enjoyment of a refurbished River Tyne for leisure, the establishment of a city centre area of advanced technology, and the encouragement of research facilities in the ship-building industry. Our agricultural hinterland, allied to the invigorating presence of ICI on Teesside, and the Department of Agriculture in Newcastle University, should provide a pointer to other research advances we must make.

As an international medical centre, I would also commend a physical link between an expanding Medical School and the city's General Hospital, and an exploitation of this potential by those industries involved in surgical and medical technologies, and located in the city's technological complex. And, of course, integrating all these, there would be a network of communications in accord with the times. 'But what about the people?' you say. 'Is it to be all planning and organization and whiter-than-white efficiency?' Of course it is not. The dignity of the individual must at all times be nurtured. It is on his behalf that planning is undertaken. He must remain the highest common factor in any decision-making. His heritage is also of importance. In order to achieve a quicker journey from Newcastle to London, and at the same time avoid catching influenza on a draughty platform, there is no need to demolish our quite precious Central Station. We can look ahead, and over our shoulder, at the same time.

The development of our Town Moor could be a case in point.

All Geordies are jealous of their city lung, almost one thousand acres in extent, to which they have access. But how many of them exercise their privilege? Precious few, it would seem, except once a year at the hoppings. I would like to see the wide open spaces remain, but made more attractive so that they would tempt people. Discreet landscaping could, in my opinion, achieve this. Let us, at any rate, ask the people. Let us ensure also that they can continue to enjoy the wonderful amenities of our coastline. To plan that this should happen is not to envisage commercial despoliation, but rather the opposite— it is to mount a deliberate preservation campaign.

What I have suggested for Newcastle as a regional capital is entirely practical. It does, however, require bold decisions. It also demands a clear relationship in the educational sector between the polytechnics, further education, secondary education and so on through to the infants' school. It also requires a new form of integration of region, town and gown. If we are going to succeed in the pursuit of these objectives, there will be necessary an understanding by education and industry and local government of the role that each has to fulfil separately and in concert, in order to aspire to new economic objectives. It then requires equally the understanding by town and gown of the importance of architectural planning. Only then can we continue to have expressed on the ground the equivalent of the enlightened research and development which will be going on towards the end of the century.

The same pattern can be repeated on Wearside, in a different form, because that area has different expressions of potential excellence. So too on Teesside. I would see, broadly speaking, a new Teesside University, and these three main centres of local government linked to educational establishments in their particular localities, receiving a feedback from the Peterlee Science Base. The prospect is exciting. But it requires discussion now. It could so easily be another of those that got away.

Like the last Labour government for instance! As a life-long socialist I cannot but regret that the Labour Party lost power

in June 1970. At the same time, Tories like Lord Hailsham and
Ted Heath have contributed to our thinking in the North, and
it is, anyhow, up to regional bodies to carry on a dialogue with
governments of all political shades. It is the message, rather
than the medium, which counts.

Finally, in trying to stand back from myself and look in on
my own character, make-up and aspirations, what can I see as
having 'got away'? It is difficult to be objective about a thing
like this. Disappointments crowd thick and fast on any individual. If I were to say that I am visually affronted every
time I look along the hotch-potch of John Dobson Street in
Newcastle, it would be tantamount to embarking on a mile-long
list of petty niggles. Rather must I concentrate on the subject of
my public life in general. What has prompted me to spend such
a lot of time, and so much energy on it? If I had devoted the
equivalent amount of time and energy to my business interests,
I might by now be a rich man, but when my will is published
I'll laugh all the way to hell. So what has motivated me? Three
things, I believe. The desire to serve, the challenge presented
by problems, and my interest in people. As a servant I have tried
in a genuine way to assess the needs of those who have placed
their confidence in me. From my Walker constituents, through
to the three million Northerners who come under the aegis of
the Northern Economic Planning Council, I have attempted to
work and fight for what seemed to be the common good. Along
the line I have made enemies, because I have never been a
man to give up. I have also been taken for a ride on many
occasions. I tend to trust people, and I am a forgiving man.
Perhaps these qualities sit uneasily on a public servant.

Problems are my *metier* because they demand solutions.
Although my elementary schools never made a scholar of me,
they must have somehow cultivated in me a penchant for
sniffing out the impossible and making it work. In my opinion,
obstacles are there to be overcome. But not by prayer; or by
speech-making; or even by sitting down in the road. One has
to use the established power structure of our democracy in

order to actually get things done. And here again, I have found myself exposed to accusations of graft and corruption in my public life, whereas I can vouch for the fact that during all my time with the Newcastle City Council, and later at Wellbar House, there can have been no cleaner administrations in Britain. Getting things done is not synonymous with pulling a fast one.

My interest in people has been a highly motivating factor in my public career. Human relationships provide the framework of experience which gives everything real meaning. Knowing and liking people enables one to put principle before power· And if some people have responded by thinking the worst of me, I can only repeat that I bear no ill-will towards them, or indeed towards anyone.

So while I have found my public life enriching, because it contains those ingredients which are dear to my heart, and concurrent with my interests, I have to admit that something got away. That 'something' was the sensitive part of me which wanted to be understood. Not thanked, or reverenced or liked. Just understood.

Some day I will have to write a book about it.